45p

OBJECTIVE TESTS IN ENGLISH LANGUAGE

B. Rowe BA

Senior Lecturer in English
Maria Assumpta College of Education
London W8

R. A. Banks MA PHD

Head of the English Department
The College of S. Mark and S. John
London SW10

University of London Press Ltd

ISBN 0 340 06522 2

First published 1970
Second edition 1971: third impression 1972

University of London Press Ltd
St Paul's House, Warwick Lane, London EC4P 4AH

Printed in Great Britain by
Hazell Watson and Viney Ltd, Aylesbury, Bucks

INTRODUCTION

The most important aim of this book is to provide a valuable year's English work in the classroom. It will have failed, in the authors' view, if it becomes merely a set of mechanical exercises for giving examination candidates some experience of the lay-out of multiple-choice questions and practice in answering objective tests as part of their preparation for GCE examinations in English Language. The passages have been selected because they seem of sufficient worth in themselves to offer students pleasure in their reading, increased sensitivity in their response to language, and greater depth in their discussions as they consider the items and the correctness of their keys.

Nevertheless, the tests are also dedicated to helping those who are preparing at school, in college, or privately, to take GCE or other examinations where the whole or part of the test will take the form of objective, multiple-choice questions. Skill in the technique of summarizing and the ability to write well will still be required of those taking examinations in English Language and will be tested by methods other than those used in objective tests. Where, however, multiple-choice questions are introduced in examinations to assess a candidate's comprehension of a given passage, as in the GCE (Ordinary Level) examination in English Language of the University of London from the summer of 1972 onwards, they will carry an important percentage of the total marks available for the whole paper.

Each comprehension exercise tested by multiple-choice questions will usually consist of two parts, as in this book. The first part will be based on the careful reading of a literary passage and the second part on the understanding of an extract of a more factual kind. The questions which follow each of the passages are called *items*. Each item consists of a *stem*, which is an introductory question, direction, or incomplete statement, and five suggested answers called the *responses* or the *options*. Only one of these options, the *key*, is the correct or best answer to the problem or question posed in the stem; the remaining options, which are incorrect or less appropriate, are called *distractors*. The items are all related to important aspects of the subject matter and its presentation and set out to test the student's ability to remember, understand, and think. The options sometimes require him to discriminate between not only right and wrong responses but also the good and the best or the probable and the most probable.

Before the items are attempted it is important that the passage on which they are based should be read several times and its general framework be understood. The *key* to each item can be found most easily by (1) reading the *stem* carefully until its requirements are clear and (2) relating the stem to the context to which it refers. The five *options* can then be considered and evaluated

Once the *key* has been finally selected the appropriate letter (**A, B, C, D,** or **E**) for the item can then be deleted on the separate answer sheet available. It is important that a student should not try to arrive at the key by guesswork. In any case, a formula to allow for guessing is built into the method used by examining bodies to assess the final results in order to eliminate any advantage that might be gained by a candidate who happens to guess correctly. If any item seems too difficult, time should not be lost by puzzling over it for too long. It is best to move on to the next and come back to the difficult one later if time allows.

As an example of the objective testing of the understanding of a passage, the following paragraph might be considered; it is selected from *New Test Papers in English Language* by Brian Rowe (University of London Press, 1967), page 31, lines 1–8:

> On the evening of the ball, Denry knew that a dress-suit is merely the beginning of anxiety. Shirt! Collar! Tie! Studs! Cuff-links! Gloves! Handkerchief! (He was very glad to learn authoritatively from Shillitoe that handkerchiefs were no longer worn in the waistcoat opening, and that men who so wore them were barbarians and the truth was not in them. Thus, an everyday handkerchief would do.) Boots! . . . Boots were the rock on which he had struck.
>
> (Arnold Bennett, *The Card*)

In comprehension tests set for GCE examinations before the introduction of multiple-choice items the following questions on the passage might have appeared:

1 Give in a single word or short phrase the meaning of the following word *as used in the passage*:
   authoritatively (line 3)

2 In what ways is a dress-suit 'merely the beginning of anxiety' for Denry (lines 1–2)?

3 Explain the following phrase briefly:
   the rock on which he had struck (lines 6–7)

Multiple-choice items could test the same material in the following ways:

1 'authoritatively' (line 3) can best be replaced by
   A dictatorially
   B arbitrarily
   C legally
   ***D** conclusively
   E genuinely

4

2 The dress-suit is 'merely the beginning of anxiety' for Denry (lines 1-2) because he

   A still had not paid for it
   B felt inferior to other guests
  ***C** found the accessories equally troublesome
   D was nervous about the coming ball
   E could not really afford to pay for the tickets

3 'The rock on which he had struck' (lines 6–7) suggests that Denry is being compared with a

  ***A** ship
   B cyclist
   C aeroplane
   D guitarist
   E ploughman

The keys are marked with an asterisk. The distractors may offer themselves as the most probable or correct answers to those who have not read the passage or the stems carefully enough, or to those who cannot distinguish shades of meaning. For example, in item 1 'conclusively' suggests that Shillitoe's well-supported experience can be trusted and accepted without further argument; 'dictatorially', on the other hand, suggests that Shillitoe has imperiously commanded Denry to obey him; 'arbitrarily' suggests that Shillitoe has made up his mind impulsively for no reason at all; whilst 'legally' and 'genuinely' introduce aspects of *authority* irrelevant in this context. Therefore, **D** can be positively identified as the key and the other options can be rejected.

It can be seen from these examples, perhaps, that multiple-choice questions can test material that was once examined in GCE papers by more traditional approaches. The fact that there is only one acceptable key to an item can focus the candidate's ability to remember, understand or think; moreover, his ability can be objectively assessed and accurately marked.

Each test in this book is designed so that the literary or the factual part can be completed within 40 minutes, the amount of time usually available for candidates to answer a comprehension exercise in class. As an assessment test, it is clearly important that the items on a passage should be completed at one sitting within a rigid time-framework but teachers who prefer to use a test as the basis for discussion will find it very easy to divide the items so that they can spend considerably longer than 40 minutes on a passage and its deeper evaluation.

B. R.
R. A. B.

MARKING THE TESTS

Answer sheets and a set of transparent marking templates (one for each test) are available with the textbook. On the answer sheets pupils cross through the numbered item responses they consider correct. The teacher then checks the total of those which agree with the appropriate test template by laying it over the answer sheet. The number of correct responses can quickly be read off and recorded in the space provided on the answer sheet.

TESTS

TEST 1

Answer all questions. Do not guess.

Passage One

Over the fence of the spinney was the hillside, scattered with old thorn trees.
'If I were a man,' said Lettie, 'I would go out west and be free. I should love it.'
   'Well—you're not a man', George said, looking at her, and speaking with
timid bitterness.

5   'No,' she laughed, 'if I were, I would shape things—oh, wouldn't I have
my own way!'
   'And don't you now?'
   'Oh—I don't want it particularly—when I've got it. When I've had my
way, I do want somebody to take it back from me.' She put her head back,

10   and looked at him sideways, laughing through the glitter of her hair. They
came to the kennels. She sat down on the edge of the great stone water trough,
and put her hands in the water, moving them gently like submerged flowers
through the clear pool. 'I love to see myself in the water,' she said, 'I don't
mean on the water, Narcissus—but that's how I should like to be out west,

15   to have a little lake of my own, and swim quite free in the water.'
   'Do you swim well?' he asked.
   'Fairly.'
   'I would race you—in your little lake.'
   He pulled his watch out of his breeches' pocket; it was half-past three.

20   'What are you looking at the time for?' she asked.
   'Meg's coming to tea', he replied. She said no more, and they walked slowly
on. When they came on to the shoulder of the hill, and looked down on to
the mill, and the mill-pond, she said: 'I will not come down with you—I will
go home.'

25   'Not come down to tea!' he exclaimed, full of reproach and amazement.
'Why, what will they say?'
   'No, I won't come down—let me say farewell. Do you remember how
Eurydice sank back into Hell?'
   'But—', he stammered, 'you must come down to tea—how can I tell them?

30   Why won't you come?'
   As she watched him, she pitied his helplessness, and gave him a last cut
as she said, very softly and tenderly: 'It wouldn't be fair to Meg.'
   He stood looking at her; his face was coloured only by the grey-brown tan;
his eyes, the dark, self-mistrustful eyes of the family, were darker than ever,

35   dilated with the misery of helplessness.
   The wood was high and warm. Along the ridings the forget-me-nots were
knee deep, stretching, glimmering into the distance like the Milky Way through
the night. They left the tall, flower-tangled paths to go in among the blue-
bells, breaking through the close-pressed flowers and ferns till they came to

8

40 an oak which had fallen across the hazels, where they sat half screened. The hyacinths drooped magnificently with an overweight of purple, or they stood pale and erect, like unripe ears of purple corn. Heavy bees swung down in a blunder of extravagance among the purple flowers. They were intoxicated even with the sight of so much blue. The sound of their hearty, wanton
45 humming came clear upon the solemn boom of the wind overhead. The sight of their clinging, clambering riot gave satisfaction to the soul.

'If there were fauns and hamadryads!' she said softly, turning to him to soothe his misery. She took his cap from his head, ruffled his hair, saying: 'If you were a faun, I would put roses round your hair, and make you look
50 Bacchanalian.' She looked up at the sky. Its blue looked pale and green in comparison with the purple tide ebbing about the wood. The clouds rose up like towers, and something had touched them into beauty, and poised them up among the winds. The clouds passed on, and the pool of sky was clear.

'Look,' she said, 'how we are netted down—boughs with knots of green
55 buds. If we were free on the winds!—But I'm glad we're not.' She turned suddenly to him, and with the same movement, she gave him her hand, and he clasped it in both his. 'I'm glad we're netted down here; if we were free in the winds—Ah!' She laughed a peculiar little laugh, catching her breath.

'Look!' she said, 'it's a palace, with the ash-trunks smooth like a girl's
60 arm, and the elm-columns, ribbed and bossed and fretted, with the great steel shafts of beech, all rising up to hold an embroidered care-cloth over us; and every thread of the care-cloth vibrates with music for us, and the little broidered birds sing; and the hazel-bushes fling green spray round us, and the honeysuckle leans down to pour out scent over us. Look at the harvest of
65 blue-bells—ripened for us! Listen to the bee, sounding among all the organ-play—if he sounded exultant for us!' She looked at him, with tears coming up into her eyes, and a little, winsome, wistful smile hovering round her mouth. He was very pale, and dared not look at her. She put her hand in his, leaning softly against him. He watched, as if fascinated, a young thrush with
70 full pale breast who hopped near to look at them—glancing with quick, shining eyes.

'The clouds are going on again', said Lettie. 'Look at that cloud face—see—gazing right up into the sky. The lips are opening—he is telling us something—now the form is slipping away—it's gone—come, we must go too.'

75 'No,' he cried, 'don't go—don't go away.'

Her tenderness made her calm. She replied in a voice perfect in restrained sadness and resignation. 'No, my dear, no. The threads of my life were untwined; they drifted about like floating threads of gossamer; and you didn't put out your hand to take them and twist them up into the chord with
80 yours. Now another has caught them up, and the chord of my life is being twisted, and I cannot wrench it free and untwine it again—I can't. I am not strong enough. Besides, you have twisted another thread far and tight into your chord; could you get free?'

'Tell me what to do—yes, if you tell me.'

85 'I can't tell you—so let me go.'

1 Lettie's hands in the water are said to resemble 'submerged flowers' (line 12) because they are

   A white
   B small
   C fragile
   D star-shaped
   E swaying

2 Lettie refers to Narcissus (line 14) because he

   A admired his own reflection
   B possessed his own lake
   C had gone to live in 'the west'
   D was a legendary swimmer
   E and Lettie resembled the flower

3 'dilated' (line 35) means

   A pleased
   B huge
   C enlarged
   D small
   E saddened

4 The forget-me-nots are said to resemble the Milky Way (line 37) because they are

   I shining softly
   II soft and white
   III in the dark
   IV thickly clustered
   V sweet-smelling

   A I and II only
   B I and IV only
   C II and III only
   D III and IV only
   E IV and V only

5 Lettie exclaims 'If there were fauns and hamadryads!' (line 47) because she

   A is becoming impatient for these birds to appear in the woodland
   B feels that the woodland is incomplete without these fairies
   C collects these colourful woodland butterflies
   D loves these small animals of the woodland
   E likes to gather these pretty woodland flowers

6 The sky above the wood looks 'pale and green' (line 50) in comparison with the

A passing clouds
B distant horizon
C woodland flowers
D nearby hills
E encircling trees

7 If the sky is a pool (line 53) the clouds are
A rocks
B froth
C waterlilies
D nets
E ripples

8 Lettie describes the tree branches (lines 54–5) as
  I unsightly
 II displeasing
III protecting
IV restrictive
 V unmingled

A I and II only
B II and III only
C III and IV only
D IV and V only
E V and I only

9 Lettie is glad that they are not 'free on the winds' (line 55) because they would
A be frozen to death
B look utterly ridiculous
C be badly hurt eventually
D forget their responsibilities
E die of suffocation

10 Lettie says that the 'palace' (line 59) contains
  I strong pillars
 II beautiful windows
III stately towers
IV rich perfumes
 V exquisite tapestries

A I, II and III only
B I, III and IV only
C I, IV and V only
D II, III and IV only
E II, IV and V only

continue overleaf

11 The trees in the wood are all of the following EXCEPT

A leafy

B large

C grooved

D interlaced

E knobbly

12 Lettie's description of the woodland (lines 59–66) can best be described as

A pompous

B pretentious

C fanciful

D uninspired

E outrageous

13 The birds are described as 'broidered' (line 63) because they are

A colourful

B artificial

C tuneful

D quivering

E distant

14 'exultant' (line 66) means

A enraptured

B inquisitive

C infuriated

D melodious

E dignified

15 The cloud (line 72) is most probably about to tell them that they

A should now leave for home

B have short fleeting lives

C must remain calm

D are insignificant creatures

E should watch the sky

16 Which of the following expressions is figurative?

A 'they came on to the shoulder of the hill' (line 22)

B 'his face was coloured only by the grey-brown tan' (line 33)

C 'along the ridings the forget-me-nots were knee deep' (lines 36–7)

D 'breaking through the close-pressed flowers and ferns' (line 39)

E 'glancing with quick shining eyes' (lines 70–1)

17 'another thread' (line 82) stands for

   A Lettie

   B George

   C Narcissus

   D Eurydice

   E Meg

18 Which of the following phrases best sums up George's feelings throughout the passage

   A 'timid bitterness' (line 4)

   B 'reproach and amazement' (line 25)

   C 'self-mistrustful' (line 34)

   D 'the misery of helplessness' (line 35)

   E 'as if fascinated' (line 69)

19 Throughout the passage Lettie's character emerges as all the following EXCEPT

   A perverse

   B compassionate

   C intelligent

   D submissive

   E imaginative

20 The main subject of this passage is the

   A beauty of the woodlands

   B relationship between Lettie and George

   C gaiety of Lettie

   D ruefulness of George

   E happiness of the woodland creatures

Passage Two

In almost all cases the soft parts of fossils are gone for ever but they were fitted around or within the hard parts. Many of them also were attached to the hard parts and usually such attachments are visible as depressed or elevated areas, ridges, or grooves, smooth or rough patches on the hard parts.

5 The muscles most important for the activities of the animal and most evident in the appearance of the living animal are those attached to the hard parts and possible to reconstruct from their attachments. Much can be learned about a vanished brain from the inside of the skull in which it was lodged.

Restoration of the external appearance of an extinct animal has little or no
10 scientific value. It does not even help in inferring what the activities of the living animal were, how fast it could run, what its food was, or such other conclusions as are important for the history of life. However, what most people want to know about extinct animals is what they looked like when they were alive. Palaeontologists also would like to know. Things like fossil
15 shells present no great problem as a rule, because the hard parts are external when the animal is alive and the outer appearance is actually preserved in the fossils. The colour is usually guesswork, although colour bands and patterns are occasionally preserved even in very ancient fossil shells.

Animals in which the skeleton is internal present great problems of restora-
20 tion, and honest restorers admit that they often have to use considerable guessing. The general shape and contours of the body are fixed by the skeleton and by muscles attached to the skeleton, but surface features, which may give the animal its really characteristic look, are seldom restorable with any real probability of accuracy. The present often helps to interpret the past. An
25 extinct animal presumably looked more or less like its living relatives, if it has any. This, however, may be quite equivocal. Extinct members of the horse family are usually restored to look somewhat like the most familiar living horses—domestic horses and their closest wild relatives. It is, however, possible and even probable that many extinct horses were striped like zebras.
30 Others probably had patterns no longer present in any living members of the family. If lions and tigers were extinct they would be restored to look exactly alike. No living elephants have much hair and mammoths, which are extinct elephants, would doubtless be restored as hairless if we did not happen to know that they had thick, woolly coats. We know this only because mammoths
35 are so recently extinct that prehistoric men drew pictures of them and that the hide and hair have actually been found in a few specimens. For older extinct animals we have no such clues. Length of hair, length and shape of ears, colour and colour pattern, presence or absence of a camel-like hump are

14

uncertain inferences at best and downright guesses at worst in most restora-
40 tions of fossils, especially those of mammals.

Without attempting a restoration much may be learned about the life activities of ancient animals from their hard parts, from shells and other external supports or from reconstructed internal skeletons. In fact even single teeth or parts of dentition or skeletons too incomplete for reconstruction may
45 permit some valid and useful inferences about the living animals. For example, food habits of extinct mammals can be judged in a general way and sometimes very specifically from their teeth. Most fossil mammals with well-developed canine teeth and shearing posterior teeth ate meat by preference. If they had sharp, large canines, only moderately heavy or light jaws and
50 posterior teeth, and had swiftly running or leaping forms they were predacious. If the teeth were heavier and blunter, the jaws more powerful, and the limbs less agile, they probably ate carrion. Mammals with low-crowned teeth and fairly numerous, non-shearing tooth points or cusps generally were omnivorous. Mammals with some sort of cropping apparatus at the front end of the
55 jaws and with heavy, rigid grinding teeth farther back ate plants. Those with relatively low teeth ate mostly leaves and twigs. Land mammals in which the teeth tended to degenerate or were lost altogether were for the most part those eating ants or termites.

1 'fossils' (line 1) are

   A the preserved bones of dead animals

   B ancient animals excavated by archaeologists

   C scientific reconstructions of prehistoric animals

   D carved stones or rock paintings of extinct animals

   E rocks bearing the imprinted shapes of dead animals

2 The soft parts of fossilized animals

   A can always be accurately identified

   B have always vanished without trace

   C can usually be reconstructed

   D have usually left some traces

   E can never be reconstructed

3 The muscles of a fossilized animal can sometimes be reconstructed because they were

   A preserved with the rest of the animal

   B part of the animal's skeleton

   C hard parts of the animal's body

   D fixed to the animal's skeleton

   E essential to the animal's activities

4 The reconstruction of a fossilized animal's external appearance is considered necessary in order to

   A satisfy popular curiosity

   B answer scientific questions

   C establish its activities

   D determine its eating habits

   E discover its agility and speed

5 'inferring' (line 10) means

   A outlining

   B restricting

   C suggesting

   D investigating

   E concluding

6 The original external appearance of a fossilized shell can normally be reconstructed because

   I its colour can be intelligently guessed

   II ancient rocks retain its pattern

   III its muscles were attached to the shell

   IV its hard parts were on the outside

A I and II only
B I and III only
C II and III only
D II and IV only
E III and IV only

7 Comparisons between living animals and fossilized creatures of the same family are useful because they are probably similar in
A bone-structure
B size
C skin-patterning
D coat
E general appearance

8 'equivocal' (line 26) means
A equally important
B definable
C equally loud
D deliberate
E equally doubtful

9 'probably' (line 30) is used to suggest
A possibility
B certainty
C likelihood
D incredulity
E emphasis

10 If lions and tigers became extinct scientists would restore them similarly from fossilized remains because they would be unsure about their
A internal skeletons
B skin patterns
C feeding habits
D family relationships
E muscular structure

11 Mammoths are usually reconstructed with hairy hides because
I scientists believe that mammoths once had hair
II elephants and mammoths are closely related
III fossilized remains clearly show that they had hair
IV mammoth hair has been found
V prehistoric pictures show them with hair

continue overleaf

A I and II only
B II and IV only
C III and IV only
D III and V only
E IV and V only

12 The third paragraph (lines 19–40) deals mainly with the difficulties of restoring fossilized animals which

A had complex internal structures
B had no external hard parts
C had fur-covered bodies
D have no living relatives
E belong to the horse and elephant families

13 For the study of the life of extinct mammals it is most important to have firm evidence of their

A restored appearance
B skeletal frames
C colour and colour patterns
D length of hair
E camel-like humps

14 'shearing posterior teeth' (line 48) are teeth that are

  I able to cut
 II sharply pointed
III at the back of the mouth
IV curved backwards
 V second, not milk-teeth

A I and III only
B I and V only
C II and III only
D II and IV only
E III and V only

15 Animals that were predators probably had all of the following EXCEPT

A sharp, canine teeth
B posterior teeth
C heavy teeth
D light jaws
E agile bodies

16 'carrion' (line 52) means

  A easily carried prey

  B dead animals

  C crows

  D rotten food

  E offal

17 A 'cusp' (line 53) is the crown or a tooth which does **not**

  A cut

  B grip

  C grind

  D tear

  E mince

18 'omnivorous' (lines 53–4) describes animals which eat

  A fresh meat only

  B rotten carrion only

  C nothing but plants

  D everything edible

  E all they can find

19 The vocabulary used in this passage can best be described as

  A colloquial

  B imaginative

  C allegorical

  D factual

  E scientific

20 The explanations set out in this passage are most probably intended for the

  A expert palaeontologist

  B professional historian

  C amateur geologist

  D general reader

  E sixth-form scientist

Answer all questions. Do not guess.

Passage One

'Mummy!' Calvert screamed from the doorstep as she raced up the path for the bus. 'Can't I go to *The Bandits of Sherwood Forest*?'

'No!' and she was out through the gate and the gate went bang!

'Mummy, you promised!'

5 She swept his hand away, furious at the public scene, and climbed on the bus. Then remembering that she had promised and that she must make some excuse, she added from the step of the bus:

'It's Lent. Nobody goes to movies in Lent!'

And the bus went on its way. He raced, bawling, after it until her promise
10 and his hopes were swept around the corner. The road was empty. He collapsed sobbing on the footpath. With the sobs his tummy went in and out like an engine. He tore penny-leaves from the wall. He dragged himself up and with one hand he played harp strings of misery along the wall back to the gate. He dragged his feet through the gravel of the path to make tram
15 lines. Then he went slowly into the breakfast room, where the morning paper stood up like a tent. His eyes caught the shine of the old jug on the sideboard. His daddy always called it an old jug; he would say to mummy, 'I might as well be talking to that old jug'. He surveyed the jug for a bit out of the corners of his eyes. Then he took it down—it was pink lustre outside, gold
20 inside—and he put it on the chair. He flopped down his knees before it, and said staring earnestly at the pink belly of the jug:

'O Jug! Please, O my good Jug, send me to *The Bandits of Sherwood Forest* at the Plaza.'

He looked up at the ceiling and stuck out his tongue. He looked at the jug.
25 He wagged his palms at it swiftly, a dozen times.

'Jug, gimme half a dollar.'

The next moment he had his fist in the jug, and pulled out two raffle tickets, a bottle of red pills, and a half-crown piece. In two shakes he was pelting up to the village. Billy Busher was there, floating a tin motorboat in
30 a puddle of water. He yelled, 'Busher, I got half a dollar'.

'*Bandits of Sherwood Forest*?'

'No! Busher, come on and we'll go down to the seaside.'

They marched off down the hill to the station.

Long before they came within sight of the sea they said they could smell it—
35 cool, damp, deep, salty, spumy, windy, roaring; the big green animal of the sea that opens up long white jaws to swallow you up with a swoosh and a roar, but you always run away from it just in time, jumping on the wet sand shrieking and laughing, and then you run in after it until another white

mouth curls up its jaws to eat you up and spit you out and you run away
40 shrieking again.

When the train stopped they scrambled up and out. They held on to their caps, looking at the waves thundering on the groaning gravel, and the dust of the waves in the wind, and every cement-fronted villa boarded up and shiny in the spume and wind.

45 'Come on away up to the old Crystal Café', Busher shouted into his ear, 'and we'll buy lemonade.'

In the window of the café was a big yellow-and-black notice: TO LET. A rain squall blasted down on them out of the purple sky. For a while they hugged back into the shelter of the café porch. Then Busher said in a flat voice:
50 'It's all a blooming suck-in.'

When the rain stopped they went slowly to the big tin shelter beside the railway restaurant. Every few seconds the tin roofs squeaked above the kettledrums of another downpour.

'You and your swimming!' Busher snarled. 'You and your merry-go-rounds!
55 Why didn't you come to *The Bandits of Sherwood Forest* when I asked you? And where did you get that half dollar anyway? I bet you stole it from your ma.'

Calvert told him. Busher stopped snivelling.

'Gawd! Calvert! You're after praying to the devil. You'll be damned for
60 a-a-all E-eternity!'

And he tore out his railway ticket and flung it in terror on the concrete and ran bawling out into the rain. He made his way to the bus stop, told a sad yarn to the driver and the conductor, and got carried home, gratis and in good time.

65 The rain hammered the convex roof; the wind rattled its bones; bits of paper went whispering around the corners like mice; the gutters spilled; the light faded. He heard the drums of the high tide pounding the beach. He sat there until nearly nine o'clock, not daring to stir, awaiting the train.

When he got home his father rushed at him and shouted, and his mother
70 was crying, but when they saw the cut of him they stopped. His dad called him 'old man' and undressed him on the warm hearthrug, and his mummy brought him in hot chocolate, and for the first time that day he suddenly began to cry.

1 Calvert's mother is angry as she gets on the bus (lines 5–6) primarily because she
   A has broken her promise to him
   B does not approve of breaking Lent
   C is embarrassed by their quarrel
   D has almost missed the only bus
   E cannot find a satisfactory excuse

2 Calvert's mother says that nobody goes to the movies in Lent (line 8), because it is a period when
   A cinemas are permanently closed
   B people deny themselves pleasure
   C film subjects are disgraceful
   D weather conditions are deplorable
   E dark nights create dangers

3 'her promise and his hopes were swept around the corner' (lines 9–10) implies that
   A he gave up thinking about the movies
   B his mother had agreed to his request
   C he was bowled over by the bus
   D the bus disappeared out of his sight
   E the bus had collided at the crossroads

4 'played harp strings of misery along the wall' (line 13) tells us that the boy probably
   A pulled up tall slender flowers in his evil temper
   B balanced forlornly on the parapet while playing a musical game
   C banged each of the railings to show his unhappy mood
   D dragged the fingers of one hand sadly along the bricks
   E sat on the fence wretchedly practising a small stringed instrument

5 As Calvert walks up the path (lines 14–15) he probably
   A pretended that he was a train
   B made two shallow parallel marks
   C heaped the stones into two ridges
   D left two deep intersecting tracks
   E uncovered a pair of iron rails

6 The morning paper is said to resemble a tent (lines 15–16) due mainly to its
   I shape
   II colour
   III size
   IV texture
   V function

A I and II only
B I and III only
C II and III only
D II and IV only
E III and V only

7 His father's reference to the jug when speaking to Calvert's mother (lines 17–18) implies that sometimes she did not
  A seem human
  B respond immediately
  C sit quietly
  D look pretty
  E possess money

8 'lustre' (line 19) is best replaced by
  A glaze
  B roundness
  C richness
  D splendour
  E desire

9 Calvert's behaviour before the jug (lines 22–6) is best described as an act of
  A clairvoyance
  B conjuration
  C telepathy
  D divination
  E exorcism

10 In lines 35–40 the sea is said to be all the following EXCEPT
  A chilly
  B boisterous
  C profound
  D lethal
  E saline

11 Another term for 'the dust of the waves' (lines 42–3)
  A silt
  B spindrift
  C bilge
  D alluvium
  E shingle

continue overleaf

12 There seem to be no facilities at the seaside primarily because the boys' visit is during a

- **A** close season
- **B** rainy spell
- **C** Sunday afternoon
- **D** working day
- **E** public holiday

13 A 'suck-in' (line 50) is a

- **A** disgrace
- **B** pity
- **C** tragedy
- **D** feast
- **E** fraud

14 In actuality, the kettledrums (line 53) consist of

- **A** metal containers for boiling water
- **B** small skin-covered wooden cylinders
- **C** rain on the shelter covering
- **D** waves on the beach outside
- **E** trains passing over rails nearby

15 Busher throws away his railway ticket (line 61) because he

- **A** considered it would be quicker to return by bus
- **B** wanted to get home before it grew dangerously late
- **C** could no longer stand all the wetness and boredom
- **D** was frightened of associating with Satan's companion
- **E** had a fit of bad temper whenever he was opposed

16 To judge from the passage Busher appears to be all the following EXCEPT

- **A** querulous
- **B** artful
- **C** lively
- **D** considerate
- **E** superstitious

17 The bits of paper are said to resemble mice (line 66) due mainly to their

- I quietness
- II outline
- III smallness
- IV movements
- V whiteness

A I, II and III only
B I, III and IV only
C II, III and IV only
D II, III and V only
E III, IV and V only

18 During their day at the seaside the two boys do all the following EXCEPT
   A get wet
   B become bored
   C visit the sea
   D go swimming
   E quarrel together

19 Calvert 'suddenly began to cry' (lines 72–3) due to his
   A sorrow and pain over losing his best friend
   B embarrassment and anger at his nakedness
   C frustration and temper after his miserable day
   D fear and apprehension of his coming punishment
   E relief and remorse at his parents' kindness

20 When Calvert returns home his parents display
   A vexation followed by compassion
   B distress followed by amusement
   C hostility followed by servility
   D derision followed by affability
   E arrogance followed by devotion

Passage Two

Most towns up to Elizabethan times were smaller than a modern village and each of them was built around its weekly market where local produce was brought for sale and the townsfolk sold their work to the people from the countryside and provided them with refreshment for the day. Trade was
5   virtually confined to that one day even in a town of a thousand or so people. On market days craftsmen put up their stalls in the open air whilst on one or two other days during the week the townsman would pack up his loaves, or nails, or cloth, and set out early to do a day's trade in the market of an adjoining town where, however, he would be charged a heavy toll for the privilege and
10 get a less favourable spot for his stand than the local craftsmen. Another chance for him to make a sale was to the congregation gathered for Sunday morning worship. Although no trade was allowed anywhere during the hours of the service (except at annual fair times), after church there would be some trade at the church door with departing country folk.
15   The trade of markets was almost wholly concerned with exchanging the products of the nearby countryside and the goods made by local craftsmen with the result that the genuine retail dealer had very little place. In all goods sold in the market but particularly in food retail dealing was distrusted as a kind of profiteering. Even when there was enough trade being done to afford
20 a livelihood to an enterprising man ready to buy wholesale and sell retail, town authorities were reluctant to allow it.

Yet there were plainly people who were tempted to 'forestall the market' by buying goods outside it, and to 'regrate' them, that is to resell them, at a higher price. The constantly repeated rules against these practices and the
25 endlessly recurring prosecutions mentioned in the records of all the larger towns prove that some well-informed and sharp-witted people did these things.

Nowadays, shopping hours are restricted in the interests of the retailers and not because of the scarcity of the goods. Medieval people restricted the market hours in the buyers' interests, so that every buyer should have an
30 equal chance to buy a fair share of whatever was going and also to enable the authorities to keep an eye on the transactions and make sure that no one made a corner in some commodity and forced up the price.

Every town made its own laws and if it was big enough to have craft guilds these regulated the business of their members and tried to enforce a strict
35 monopoly of their own trades. Yet while the guild leaders, as craftsmen, followed fiercely protectionist policies, at the same time, as leading townsmen, they wanted to see a big, busy market yielding a handsome revenue in various dues and tolls. Conflicts of interest led to endless, minute regulations, change-

able, often inconsistent, frequently absurd. There was a time in the fourteenth
40 century, for example, when London fishmongers were not allowed to handle
any fish that had not already been exposed for sale for three days by the
men who caught it.

In a diet where fruit and vegetables were scarce and poor, fish made a most
welcome change and the whole population ate no meat on Fridays and fast
45 days and all through Lent. Fresh fish was very dear and even salted or dried
or smoked fish, much more widely eaten, was very expensive. Salt herrings,
the cheapest and most plentiful fish, were the universal standby. People who
could afford the outlay bought their salt herring by the barrel at the autumn
fairs to store for winter and the following Lent.

1 The growth of towns before Elizabethan times was determined mainly by
   A their comparatively small size
   B their regular markets
   C centrally planned building
   D locally produced goods
   E neighbouring tradesmen

2 'virtually' (line 5) carries the force of
   A actually
   B definitely
   C practicably
   D practically
   E honestly

3 Tradesmen preferred to work in their own towns because there they could
   A easily find good refreshment
   B sell any kind of produce
   C work in the open air
   D start work very early
   E have the best placed stalls

4 If tradesmen sold their produce in towns other than their own they would
   A find profitable trade much slower
   B have to pay a special tax
   C need to start work much earlier
   D find local competition too hard
   E have a long journey to work

5 A tradesman was free to sell his goods only
   A at certain approved times
   B on special market days
   C at the annual fairs
   D on alternate Sunday mornings
   E at the end of services

6 In medieval markets there was little retail trade because
   A money was never used in sales
   B producers sold directly to consumers
   C there were no fixed positions for shops
   D craftsmen preferred wholesale trade
   E buying and selling were heavily taxed

7 The main accusation levelled against retailers was that they
  A interfered with market-trading
  B reduced the profit of craftsmen
  C charged unnecessarily high prices
  D were basically dishonest to everyone
  E restricted the trade available

8 Retailers were allowed to sell only when
  A the market was slack and empty
  B they could not make a quick profit
  C they could hardly make a livelihood
  D they had received formal approval
  E wholesalers were prepared to take a chance

9 'reluctant' (line 21) means
  A strongly persuaded
  B hardly willing
  C strictly determined
  D certainly wrong
  E under pressure

10 'forestall the market' (line 22) means
  A buy from a stall outside the market place
  B acquire goods in quantity before the market
  C have the best and the first stall in the market
  D sell at a higher price than competitors
  E gamble on profit and loss accounts

11 'recurring' (line 25) suggests that the prosecutions mentioned were
  A excessively tedious
  B judicially formal
  C frequently similar
  D seemingly unavoidable
  E essentially repetitive

12 Extant documents provide evidence of frequent illegal profit-making by giving details of

  I   regulations
  II summonses
  III affidavits
  IV bye-laws

continue overleaf

A I and II only
B I and III only
C II and III only
D II and IV only
E III and IV only

13 Times of trading were restricted essentially to protect the
A retailers
B clergymen
C wholesalers
D consumers
E authorities

14 'transactions' (line 31) means
A activities
B movements
C regulations
D cheating
E bargaining

15 Restricted trading hours enabled the authorities especially to ensure that nobody
A made a large profit
B charged high prices
C created a monopoly
D used retail methods
E employed sharp practice

16 In larger towns the craft guilds advocated
A protection rackets
B market control
C specialist trading
D tougher laws
E revision of taxes

17 A major problem for guild leaders lay in the
A divided loyalty between town and guild
B guilds' indecisiveness about retailers
C internal disagreements about taxes and dues
D hesitation over introducing guild reform
E inconsistent attitudes from the authorities

18 Sometimes craft guilds approved ridiculous measures because they
  A were not willing to reach agreement
  B wished to safeguard their positions
  C could not make satisfactory regulations
  D found market conditions too unstable
  E needed to ensure the town's prosperity

19 The least economical way to buy fish was probably to buy it
  A fresh
  B barrelled
  C salted
  D dried
  E smoked

20 If a further paragraph followed this passage it would most likely have been about
  A Elizabethan urban life
  B aspects of medieval diet
  C activities of craft guilds
  D medieval market regulations
  E the development of money in trading

TEST 3

Answer all questions. Do not guess.

Passage One

It was always to young John Shawcross a magnificent moment when the Old
Warrior got up to unhook the sabre. There was the old man, his once-large
body now a deflated sack, sagging in the chair, his head sunk upon his chest,
his great untended beard imparting an indescribable air both of grandeur and
5 ancientry, his old rheumy eyes, with red haws like a hound's turned upon
some far-back memory, his blue veined hands resting upon the chair's arms
and occasionally rising and falling as if beating the cadence of a song sung
long ago.

He was so old and done with and finished; and there was the sabre, as old
10 as he was, shining with a bright menace like a flame that might yet begin a
conflagration.

And sometimes the flame that was in the sabre would be in the old man's
eyes when occasion led him to speak of 1819. He had told the tale so often
that he never stumbled in its telling, not even now in the days of his last decrepi-
15 tude. It ran down the grooves of his memory as easily as a ship launched on a
greased slipway. He would evoke the gay break of the morning of that August
day when he was a boy of twenty, a boy in love going out to meet his girl. He
laid the sabre on the table under the lamp, and it shone with a curve of solid
light.

20 'It was like a holiday. That was the funny thing about it. It was like a
holiday to begin with: all fun, what with the bands and the singing and us
all wearing our best.'

The Old Warrior paused and held out his transparent hands to the flames,
and a look of wonder came into his eyes as though, even now, when nearly
25 sixty years were passed, he could not get over that perplexity: the gay August
morning, all fun, that was to close in so dark a night.

'Why did I do it? God have mercy on my soul, why did I do it?'

He was such a shambling, done-for simulacrum of a man that the swift
torrent of fury tearing though him and shaking him like a reed seemed to
30 come not from within him but from the dead, wellnigh forgotten years when
all those thousands lived and moved who now were gone like Emma who
died that day.

There they were, then, those thousands upon thousands of Lancashire
working folk, men, women and children, milling and shouting in the field that
35 still stood open in the heart of the town. A holiday crowd for the most part,
some of them intent, but not too seriously, on hearing what the speakers would
have to say about this improbable question of their lives being made a little
more bearable; and a few blackly set on a desperate venture.

Ah, poor Warrior! The Cap of Liberty, and one or two such symbols—see
40 that banner with the skull and crossbones!—did not look pretty to the
magistrates safely secluded in a room above the heated cheering crowd.

'We didn't know!' he cried. 'We never guessed!' But they knew then, with
the grey rounded rumps of the horses pushing among them, with the sabres
rising and falling.

45 'There were so many of us, we couldn't move, and they came at us like
mad. I thought at first they were just trying to clear us out, till I heard Emma
shriek and saw the blood rush out of her mouth as she opened it. Even with
that, her mouth spouting red, she managed to shout: 'Dragoons! Dragoons!
Get out of it!' and then she fell and they went over her. I slipped in some
50 blood and fell, and when the hoofs came pounding down I thought I was
done for. But they missed me, and I lay there for a second with the dark
arch of the horse over me. Then the horse was gone, and there was Emma,
lying on the ground.'

The old man's voice trembled. His hands trembled on the arms of the chair.
55 'She was dead. The blood was spurting out of her neck.'

He didn't speak for a moment, then he said simply: 'He had cut through
her hair at the side of her head, the bit she had tied a ribbon on. I picked it
up and put it in my pocket. There was nothing I could do for her then. I went
to find the soldier.'

60 He found him spurring his horse into a desperate mass of fustian and
corduroy, gingham and shawls and ribbon: found him with his arm again
uplifted to strike. 'I whirled my staff—and his elbow cracked like a broken
stick when I hit it.'

The Old Warrior gazed, almost with affection, at the curved, shining
65 length of steel. 'A symbol,' he said. 'Not much now to me.' Then he turned
his old head slowly towards young John Hamer Shawcross, sitting spell-
bound beside the lamp. 'But what about him, eh?' he asked. 'You've got a
long way to go, young feller. You'll see things—many strange things. A
symbol might help you to sort 'em out. Well, there's a sword from the field
70 of Peterloo.'

1 It is a magnificent moment (line 1) for John Shawcross when the Old Warrior rises to unhook the sabre because
  A the old man triumphed over his pain
  B he would be allowed to play with it
  C it became a curve of solid light
  D he knew he was in for a story
  E the old man would break into song

2 The Old Warrior's eyes are said to resemble a hound's (line 5) because they have
  A large glowing pupils
  B raw sunken sockets
  C heavily veined whites
  D sagging lower lids
  E inflamed upper lids

3 The 'conflagration' (line 11) is used figuratively for a
  A church audience
  B political revolution
  C exploding fire
  D violent argument
  E serious epidemic

4 'the flame that was in the sabre' is sometimes 'in the old man's eyes' (lines 12–13) because he is said to be
  A hot
  B feverish
  C insane
  D enchanted
  E angry

5 'decrepitude' (lines 14–15) is the state of
  A being worn out with old age
  B possessing a thin, cackling voice
  C suffering from a fatal illness
  D losing all one's teeth and hair
  E appearing rather sly and shifty

6 As it lies on the table (line 18) the sabre's most noticeable qualities are said to be its
  A size and weight
  B strength and sharpness
  C balance and delicacy
  D shape and brilliance
  E colour and beauty

7 The Old Warrior was probably born in

  A 1779

  B 1789

  C 1799

  D 1809

  E 1819

8 The old Warrior's hands are said to be transparent (line 23) because they are

  A feeble with infirmity

  B hot with fever

  C thin with age

  D trembling with cold

  E white with palsy

9 'simulacrum' line (28) is a

  A wreck

  B dwarf

  C remnant

  D image

  E silhouette

10 In lines 28–9 the effect of the Old Warrior's anger upon himself is compared with

  A a thatched roof during a violent gale

  B a wind instrument playing noisy music

  C a tall plant in rapidly moving water

  D a sharp sword plunging through flesh

  E a powerful dog shaking a dead rat

11 The magistrates (line 41) must have decided that the crowd's behaviour constituted

  A strike

  B a joke

  C an orgy

  D a riot

  E a protest

12 The crowd neither knew nor guessed, according to the Old Warrior (line 42), that

  A troops were to disperse them

  B they looked so invitingly defenceless

  C holidays could be very exciting

  D pirates had joined their numbers

  E flags were being publicly disgraced

continue overleaf

13 The incident described between line 42 and line 63 is generally known as the

A Luddite riots

B Nore mutiny

C Tolpuddle martyrs

D Peterloo massacre

E Chartist rebellion

14 The magistrates' actions turned the meeting into

A a revolution

B an execution

C an assassination

D a post-mortem

E a massacre

15 The crowd's main difficulty in trying to escape was their being

A totally unsuspecting

B without leaders

C tightly packed

D uncertain underfoot

E utterly panic-stricken

16 'Dragoons' (line 48) are

A warning sounds

B heavy cavalry

C foreign soldiers

D painful noises

E mythical reptiles

17 The crowd in lines 60–1 is mainly described in terms of

A cloth

B confusion

C animals

D fear

E machinery

18 The Old Warrior obtained the sabre by

A finding it on the field

B making it from a model

C buying it from a shop

D taking it from a soldier

E stealing it from the armoury

19 To the Old Warrior the sabre is a symbol of
  A light in darkness
  B danger in life
  C beauty in design
  D bravery in action
  E freedom from oppression

20 We are told that the immediate effect of the Old Warrior's story-telling on John Shawcross is
  A permanent
  B exciting
  C magical
  D disturbing
  E transient

Passage Two

There is a basic hypothesis that the majority of serious motoring offences are derived from accidents, and there is nothing in the offender's personality or background that predisposes him to break the law. If an accident is a chance event that happens so quickly and suddenly that it is beyond anyone's control
5 to prevent it, then it is clear that this hypothesis is disproved. For only about 14 per cent of the 653 offences considered in a recent survey could possibly be called inadvertent accidents in this sense, and even this estimate is stretching credulity to its limits. In the great majority of cases the offences were largely of the offenders' own making, and the most obvious explanation seemed to
10 be expediency in the absence of any constraints upon behaviour. In 11 per cent of the 653 cases and 21 per cent of 43 offenders who were interviewed there was evidence of selfish, and even ruthless, self-interest, but it was not possible to infer personality disturbance in more than 25 per cent of the 653 and 39 per cent of the 43 offenders. Though the inferences with regard to personality
15 traits may be an overestimate in the interpretation of qualitative data, they could equally be an underestimate, since so very little was ever recorded about the offenders themselves. The lack of data is a consequence of the almost total lack of interest in motoring offenders as persons.

It must be assumed, therefore, in the absence of evidence to the contrary
20 that the majority of serious motoring offenders considered in the survey were normal people, who succumbed to temptation when circumstances were favourable and it was expedient to take a chance, so perhaps there is something in the normal personality that predisposes a driver to break the law. Whatever it is, its presence is much more evident in males than in females, since the
25 analysis of the national statistics shows a predominance of males over females of between 18:1 and 22:1. The real significance of these figures is hard to assess, because the relative proportions of each sex at risk are unknown. One research worker produced a ratio of six males to one female from his sample of insurance policy holders, but this is almost certainly an underestimate
30 since many females—probably more than males—are likely to be driving on someone else's policy. A ratio of three to one is probably nearer to the real state of affairs. Females reached noticeable proportions only among the hit-and-run drivers, and there seems to be some justification for calling this the 'feminine' offence. The difference between the sexes in their relative
35 propensity to break the law on the roads is important, because it shows that motoring offenders have a characteristic in common with offenders in other fields of criminal activity, where males predominate to a marked degree. One motor insurance underwriter recently announced his intention to offer dis-

counts on premiums where the policy holder or the 'named driver' was a
40 woman.

The basic hypothesis is further disproved by the very high incidence, among the offences studied, of failing to insure against third-party risks. Yet accidents brought to light only a very small percentage of this kind of crime. Moreover, it could not possibly be said that this, the most common of the serious offences,
45 was brought about by providence. On the contrary, it can be regarded as a typical form of economic crime, which, although sometimes committed through inadvertence, is more usually quite deliberate and calculated .

1 'hypothesis' (line 1) means
   A wrong belief
   B unproved theory
   C demonstrable idea
   D logical argument
   E fundamental law

2 The 'basic hypothesis' discussed in the passage is that

   I accidents are, by definition, chance events
   II accidents give rise to most serious motoring offences
   III motoring offenders are not naturally criminally disposed
   IV motoring offenders have unhappy personalities and backgrounds

   A I and II only
   B I and III only
   C II and III only
   D II and IV only
   E III and IV only

3 The 'basic hypothesis' cannot be maintained if it is shown that

   I inadequate third-party insurance is a common offence
   II women drivers have fewer serious accidents than men
   III something in the character of normal drivers makes them law-breakers
   IV accidents can be prevented by less selfishness on the road

   A I and II only
   B I and III only
   C II and III only
   D II and IV only
   E III and IV only

4 'inadvertent' (line 7) means
   A insignificant
   B unnoticed
   C uncontrollable
   D illegal
   E unacceptable

5 'stretching credulity to its limits' (lines 7–8) suggests that the estimate given is
   A as generous as possible
   B impossible to believe
   C strictly interpreted
   D far too optimistic
   E deliberately falsified

40

6 From the statistics given about the personalities of motoring offenders it is clear that

   A most drivers are selfish and thoughtless

   B half the drivers are seriously disturbed

   C ruthlessness causes most accidents

   D character cannot be accurately assessed

   E nothing really definite can be concluded

7 Inadequate statistical information about the personalities of motoring offenders is largely the result of

   A the difficulty of interpreting facts

   B the inaccessibility of police records

   C lack of official concern about them as people

   D scanty recorded evidence of their offences

   E insufficient research into qualitative data

8 'traits' (line 15) means

   A layers

   B improvements

   C deficiencies

   D characteristics

   E disturbances

9 'the analysis of national statistics' (lines 24–5) shows conclusively that

   A there are twenty times more men drivers than women drivers

   B more motoring offences are committed by men than by women

   C men are essentially more evil than women

   D men take far more risks than women

   E men find it harder to resist temptation than women

10 The evidence about motoring offenders in the analysis of national statistics is

   A incomplete

   B incomprehensible

   C inaccurate

   D distorted

   E valueless

11 It is unreliable to assess the numbers of women drivers from the number of policy-holders because

   A not all women drivers hold policies

   B some women drive without insurance

   C companies are reluctant to insure women

   D only husbands need to hold insurance policies

   E women usually drive someone else's car

continue overleaf

12 The commonest serious motoring offence committed by women seems to be the failure to

A take out proper insurance

B drive with due care

C give way to pedestrians

D stop after an accident

E observe traffic signals

13 'propensity' (line 35) means

A refusal

B reluctance

C inclination

D determination

E ability

14 Women can sometimes get more favourable motoring insurance terms than men because statistically they are

A much better at controlling a car

B numerically smaller and unimportant

C less inclined to have serious accidents

D less likely to commit grave offences

E unwilling to take out policies themselves

15 A 'named driver' (line 39) is one who is

A accident-prone

B the third party in an accident

C wanted by the police

D expressly covered by the policy

E able to drive though uninsured

16 'incidence' (line 41) means

A chance of prosecution

B number of cases

C rate of occurrence

D possibility of coincidence

E element of risk

17 A 'third party' (line 42) is essentially

A any insured woman driver

B the driver of the insured car

C any other road-user

D the normal policy-holder

E the insurance company

18 'inadvertence' (line 47) suggests that some who fail to take out proper legal insurance are
   A careless
   B criminal
   C in hard straits
   D dishonest
   E forgetful

19 The main discussion of this passage is largely
   A meditative
   B analytical
   C descriptive
   D satirical
   E apologetic

20 The subject of the whole passage is best summed up by the phrase
   A the law and criminal road offences
   B the insurance of motor vehicles
   C the causes of road accidents
   D the faults of men and women drivers
   E the personality of motoring offenders

TEST 4

Passage One

When mother was no better in the morning I went to Minnie Ryan.

'I'd get the doctor at once', she said firmly.

To get the doctor I had to go first to the house of a Poor Law Guardian for a ticket to show we couldn't pay, and then to the dispensary. After that I had
5 to rush back, to get the house ready and prepare a basin of water, soap and towel for the doctor to wash his hands.

He didn't come until after dinner. He was supposed to be 'the cleverest man in Cork if only he'd mind himself'. To judge from the way he looked he hadn't been minding himself much that morning.

10 'How are you going to get this prescription now?' he growled. 'The only place open is the North Dispensary.'

'I'll go, doctor', I said at once.

I didn't think myself he could be a very good doctor, because, after all my trouble he never washed his hands.

15 The road to the dispensary led uphill past the school. The schoolhouse and the sloping yard were like a picture, except for the chorus of poor victims through the opened windows, and a glimpse of Danny Delaney's bald pate as he did sentry-go near the front door with his cane behind his back. That was grand. The pathway then dropped away to the bank of a little
20 stream where a brewery stood, and from that, far beneath you, the opposite hillside, a murmuring honeycomb of houses whose noises came to you, dissociated and ghostlike, rose to the gently rounded top with a tall limestone spire and a squat purple sandstone tower rising out of it. It was so wide a view that it was never all lit up together; the sunlight wandered across it as across a prairie.

25 The dispensary was a sordid hallway with a bench to one side and a window like a railway ticket office at the end. There was a little girl with a green plaid shawl about her shoulders sitting on the bench. She was a nice, talkative little girl and I never noticed the time till the shutter went up and a bottle was banged down on the counter.

30 'Here you are, Dooley!' shouted the seedy man and the window shut again.

'Give us a taste of your bottle, little boy', she said.

'Can't you taste your own?' I replied suspiciously.

'Ah, mine is awful', she said with a mournful shrug. 'Tonics is awful. Try it, if you like.'

35 I did, and hastily spat it out. But after that, I couldn't do less than let her taste mine. She took a long swig out of it that alarmed me.

'That's grand!' she said enthusiastically. 'I love cough bottles. Try yourself and see.'

I did, and saw that she was right about that too. It was very sweet and
40 sticky, like treacle, only with more bite in it.

'Give us another', she said, grabbing at it.

'I will not', I said in alarm. "Twill be all gone.'

'Ah, don't be an old miser', she said scornfully, with a curious pout. 'You
have gallons of it.'

45 And somehow I couldn't refuse her. My mother was far away, and I was
swept from anchorage into an unfamiliar world of spires and towers, trees,
steps and little girls with red hair and green eyes.

'It's nearly all gone', I said, beginning to snivel. 'What am I going to do
now?'

50 'Finish it and say the cork fell out', she replied as though it were the most
natural thing in the world, and I believed her. We finished it between us, and
then gradually as I put down the empty bottle I remembered my mother sick
and my heart sank. I had sacrificed her to a little girl, and she didn't even
care for me. Too late I saw her guile and burst into tears.

55 Then I crawled miserably back over the hill. All the light had gone out of
the day, and the echoing hillside had become a vast alien, cruel world. As
well as that I felt terribly sick after the cough bottle. It even crossed my mind
they I might die myself. In one way it would be a great ease to me.

Mother was still in bed. I couldn't bear it, and I began to howl.

60 'What is it, child?' my mother cried anxiously from upstairs.

'I drank all the medicine', I bellowed from the foot of the stairs and then
dashed blindly up and buried my face in the bedclothes.

'Oh, wisha, you poor misfortunate child!' she cried in relief, running her
hand through my hair. 'You poor child! Going all that way by yourself,
65 without a proper dinner, and then to have your journey for nothing. Undress
yourself now and rest here for a while.'

She rose, put on her slippers and her overcoat and unlaced my boots while
I sat on the bed. Even before she was finished I was fast asleep. Some time
later I felt a hand on my forehead and saw Minnie Ryan peering down at me,
70 laughing.

1 The main function of the Poor Law Guardian (line 3) is obviously to
  A protect children
  B maintain order
  C provide money
  D dispense charity
  E prepare medicine

2 'mind' (line 8) means
  A object to
  B listen to
  C look after
  D believe in
  E work for

3 The boy's low estimation of the doctor's medical ability is based on the doctor's apparent

   I lateness of arrival
  II untidiness of appearance
 III dislike of children
  IV gruffness of voice
   V lack of hygiene

  A I and II only
  B I and V only
  C II and III only
  D II and V only
  E III and IV only

4 'the chorus of poor victims' (lines 16–17) refers to
  A actors
  B choirboys
  C pupils
  D soldiers
  E convicts

5 Danny Delaney (line 17) appears to be a
  A teacher
  B soldier
  C prefect
  D pensioner
  E policeman

6 The houses on the opposite hillside below the boy (lines 19–23) remind him most of the

    A flurry around a coral reef
    B fuss of a ladies' hairdresser's
    C tumult in a toffee factory
    D bustle of a confectionery shop
    E activity inside a busy beehive

7 'dissociated' (lines 21–2) means

    A obscured
    B unconnected
    C faded
    D ignored
    E destroyed

8 The spire and tower (lines 22–3) are contrasted in all of the following ways EXCEPT

    A colour
    B shape
    C material
    D position
    E size

9 The view mainly reminds the author of a prairie (line 24) because of its

    A colour
    B vegetation
    C flatness
    D silence
    E breadth

10 The dispenser's window (lines 25–6) resembles that of a railway ticket office because it

    I opens on to another room
    II tickets are issued there
    III has a cover for its aperture
    IV possesses a ledge beneath it
    V entails a long wait there

    A I, II and III only
    B I, III and IV only
    C II, III and IV only
    D II, III and V only
    E III, IV and V only

continue overleaf

11 'seedy' (line 30) means

    A shabby

    B tiny

    C mature

    D thin

    E smelly

12 In her attempts to drink Dooley's medicine the little girl used all the following successfully EXCEPT

    A disdain

    B strength

    C cunning

    D charm

    E veracity

13 Dooley allows his mother's medicine to be drunk for all the following reasons EXCEPT that he

    A enjoys its flavour very much

    B feels sorry for the girl

    C is far from his home

    D overestimates the bottle's capacity

    E becomes deluded by the girl

14 In the statement 'I was swept from anchorage' (lines 45–6) it is implied that

    A the girl is a mermaid and the boy a sailor

    B the mother is a ship and the area a rock

    C the girl is a cargo and the area a ship

    D the boy is a boat and his mother a shelter

    E the boy is a tide and the area a dock

15 The statement 'I had sacrificed her to a little girl' (line 53) means that the boy had

    A been a mother to the girl

    B given the medicine to the girl

    C put himself out for the girl

    D fallen in love with the girl

    E harmed his mother and the girl

16 Dooley felt that dying would be 'a great ease' (line 58) because it would free him from

    A lovesickness

    B girls

    C remorse

    D walking

    E ghosts

17 The reaction of Dooley's mother on his return home from the dispensary is best described as one of

A composure
B complaining
C compromise
D complacency
E compassion

18 Dooley buries his face in the bedclothes (line 62) because he feels

  I angry
 II exhausted
III ashamed
IV unwell
 V unsightly

A I, II and III only
B II, III and IV only
C III, IV, and V only
D IV, V, and I only
E V, III and II only

19 Minnie Ryan's hand is on Dooley's forehead (line 69) in order to
A soothe his pain
B calm his dreams
C feel for injuries
D test for fever
E tidy his hair

20 Minnie Ryan is probably laughing (line 70) at the

  I boy's adventure
 II mother's remarks
III boy's illness
IV mother's appearance
 V boy's appearance

A I, II and III only
B I, II and IV only
C I, II and V only
D II, III and IV only
E III, IV and V only

Passage Two

At the beginning of 1918 Germany and Austria were at war with Britain and France. By the end of 1939 Germany and Austria (then one country) were again at war with Britain and France. In both world wars the U.S.A. remained neutral in the early years and then joined on the Allies' side; its intervention
5 on both occasions made a decisive contribution to the Allied victory. In the First World War Russia fought alongside Britain and France until the revolution of 1917; in the Second World War Russia remained neutral until Hitler gratuitously invaded it in 1941. Both wars are commonly regarded as struggles between Britain—or Britain and France—and Germany; yet both
10 began as small-scale wars in central Europe, following Austria's attack on Serbia and Germany's on Poland.

By the end of 1937 the principles of collective security had been thoroughly undermined. Manchuria, Abyssinia, the Rhineland, Spain—each marked a further stage in the process whereby the authority of the League of Nations
15 had been weakened and the fascist powers had gained prestige at the expense of the western democracies. The British and French governments reacted to the growing tensions in the two complementary ways of appeasement and rearmament.

The policy of appeasement was based on the assumption that the fascist
20 powers had specific and limited diplomatic aims. Its British supporters accepted Mussolini's case for Italian colonization and the nationalist arguments which Hitler employed to justify his successive violations of the Treaty of Versailles; the British, indeed, did not regard the provisions of the Versailles Treaty as fair to Germany. The appeasers believed that a sense of national
25 grievance had brought Mussolini and Hitler to power and hoped that their domestic authority would be weakened when no longer bolstered by nationalist emotions. The horror of war encouraged peace-loving peoples to deceive themselves over the dictator's intentions. The extreme right was more alarmed by communism than by fascism, while the left placed its faith in the League of
30 Nations. In practical terms, appeasement gave the western powers time to rearm, and the fact that Chamberlain had done all that could be reasonably expected and more to prevent war had the considerable advantage that when war came the British government had the backing of public opinion at home and abroad. But it had the grave disadvantages that the Austrians and
35 Czechs were sacrificed in the pursuance of the policy and that other countries, notably Russia, lost faith in the power of the western democracies to stand up to the dictators.

Rearmament was an insurance against the failure of appeasement. As early

as 1935 the British National government had launched a tentative rearmament
40 programme. An effort was made to strengthen the Royal Air Force, and radar
was developed as a possible aid to defence against bombing raids. Meanwhile
in France the Maginot Line was still more heavily fortified; the argument of
(the then) Colonel de Gaulle that only fast-moving armoured divisions could
withstand a German offensive was ignored. France's concentration upon the
45 defence of its German frontier convinced its east European allies that they
could not rely upon it for support, and Poland and the other powers started
each to look to its own security. It was these east European powers which
were directly threatened by Hitler.

1 Between 1918 and 1939 Germany and Austria
   A were at war
   B attacked France
   C became unified
   D remained neutral
   E attacked Serbia and Poland

2 The two world wars were alike in all of the following respects EXCEPT
   A they began with comparatively small invasions
   B the Germans (or Austrians) made the first moves
   C the Russians were belligerents at the start of both
   D the Americans joined both wars only once they had begun
   E the British and the French fought Germany in both

3 The Americans' role in the Allied victories can most fully be described as
   A neutral
   B interventionist
   C isolationist
   D lackadaisical
   E conclusive

4 In the First World War Russia's contribution to its allies was
   A ridiculously small
   B exceptionally strong
   C prematurely ended
   D assiduously pursued
   E successfully concluded

5 'gratuitously' (line 8) suggests that Hitler's attack on Russia was
   A unprovoked
   B fanatical
   C uninspired
   D fortuitous
   E ill-conceived

6 The use of dashes in line 9 indicates that the original idea needs to be
   A hyphenated
   B bracketed
   C questioned
   D rejected
   E qualified

7 In its analysis of 1918 and 1939 the first paragraph is mainly concerned with the two world wars and the

    A parts played by America and Russia
    B contemporary states of Europe
    C alignments of nations and peoples
    D reasons for the Allied victories
    E economic conditions leading to war

8 The second paragraph suggests that by **1938** individual nations had ceased to believe in the

    A fundamental principles of national liberty
    B League of Nations' peace-keeping ability
    C support of other nations' combined strength
    D essential sanctity of agreed national boundaries
    E military strength of democratic nations

9 'undermined' (line 13) means

    A destroyed
    B blown up
    C weakened
    D shaken
    E discredited

10 By the outbreak of the war in 1939 the Fascists had conquered all of the following EXCEPT

    A Manchuria
    B Poland
    C Spain
    D the Rhineland
    E Abyssinia

11 The success of the totalitarian armies had the immediate effect of

    I restoring the resolve of the League of Nations
    II increasing the reputation of the Fascists
    III encouraging rearmament movements
    IV reducing the overall strength of Britain

    A I and II only
    B I and III only
    C II and III only
    D II and IV only
    E III and IV only

continue overleaf

12 The use of 'complementary' (line 17) suggests that the policies of rearmament and appeasement
   A counteracted each other
   B together provided an answer
   C flattered the Fascists
   D weakened the western powers
   E supplemented other political moves

13 All of the following arguments were used by British appeasers who did not oppose the Fascists' invasions EXCEPT
   A the League of Nations was powerless
   B the dictators would finally be rejected
   C the invasions could be partially justified
   D nationalism was caused by long-standing grievances
   E the Treaty of Versailles had been unfair

14 'successive' (line 22) indicates that Hitler's violations of the Treaty of Versailles were
   A excessive
   B successful
   C repetitive
   D repeated
   E provocative

15 It is clear from the passage that the Treaty of Versailles was signed
   A in 1917
   B in 1918
   C between 1918 and 1937
   D between 1937 and 1939
   E after 1939

16 Appeasement of the Fascists was strongly advocated for all of the following reasons EXCEPT
   A communism was also a threat
   B treaties could not produce peace
   C the League of Nations still existed
   D they had no wide expansionist policies
   E war would produce untold miseries

17 The policy of appeasement was ultimately of great value mainly because it
   A gave Britain time to maintain its forces
   B encouraged the dictators to be too confident
   C showed that war was the only real solution
   D meant only the limited sacrifice of small nations
   E raised few doubts about the western powers' strength

18 The rearmament programme launched by the British National government included all of the following EXCEPT

A the reinforcement of the Maginot Line
B the development of radar stations
C the improvement of defensive measures
D better anti-aircraft precautions
E expansion of the Royal Air Force

19 Colonel de Gaulle believed that France's line of defence was particularly vulnerable because it was

A not heavily fortified
B too extensive
C begun too late
D lacking in mobility
E unsupported by armour

20 Countries in eastern Europe began to doubt the West's intentions to come to their aid if attacked because

   I Britain and France followed a policy of appeasement
  II France was mainly intent on protecting its eastern borders
 III Czechoslovakia and Poland were in imminent, direct danger
 IV Hitler was obviously about to threaten the East

A I and II only
B I and III only
C II and III only
D II and IV only
E III and IV only

TEST 5

Answer all questions. Do not guess.

Passage One

Lilian sat idle at her desk in Felix Grig's establishment in Clifford Street, off Bond Street. Lilian's lamp was lighted, and she sat alone, with darkness above her chestnut hair and about her, and a circle of radiance below. She was twenty-three. Through the drawn blind of the window could just be
5 discerned the backs of the letters of words painted on the glass:

FELIX GRIG. *Typewriting Office. Open day and night.*

That a beautiful young girl, created for affection and expensive flattery, should be sitting by herself at 11 p.m. in a gloomy office in Clifford Street, in the centre of the luxurious, pleasure-mad, love-mad West End of London
10 seemed shocking and contrary to nature, and Lilian certainly so regarded it. She pictured the shut shops, and shops and yet again shops, filled with elegance and costliness—robes, hats, stockings, shoes, gloves, furs, jewels, perfumes— designed and confected for the setting-off of just such young attractiveness as hers. She pictured herself rifling those deserted and silent shops by some
15 magic means and emerging safe, undetected, in warm marvellous sables that no blast of wind or misfortune could ever penetrate—and diamonds in her hair.

Lilian was confused by a momentary magnificent, vague vision of a man framed in the doorway. The door, drawn backwards from without, hid the
20 vision. Then there was a cough. She realized with alarm that she had been asleep, or at least dozing over her machine. In the fifth of a second she was wide awake and alert.

'Who's there?' she called, steadying her voice to a matter-of-fact and casual tone.
25 The door was pushed open, and the man who had been a vision entered.

'I beg your pardon', said he. 'I wasn't sure whether it was the proper thing to come in here.'

'This is the room to come to', said Lilian, with a prim counterfeit of a smile.

'I've only just written it', said he. 'And I want it in the morning before 8.30.
30 I wonder whether you'd be good enough to do it for me.'

'Let me see', said Lilian professionally. 'About fifteen hundred words, or hardly. Oh, yes! I will do it myself.'

'Now shall I call for the copy about 8 o'clock?'

'I'm afraid the office won't be open at 8 o'clock,' said Lilian. 'We close at
35 6.30. for an hour or two. But what's the address?'

'6a Jermyn Street. You'll see it all on the back of the last page.'

'It could be delivered by 6.30 this morning, and you could take it out of

the box any time after that.' The idea seemed to have spontaneously presented itself to her. She forbore to say that her intention was to deliver the copy
40 herself on her way home.

'Well, all I say is, it's very wonderful.'

She smiled again:

'It's just our business.'

He bowed gracefully in departing.

45 As soon as he was gone she looked at the back of the last page. 'Lord Mackworth.' Never having heard of such a lord, she consulted the office *Who's Who*. Yes, he was there. What a figure! He had everything—title, blood, wealth, style, a splendid presence, perfect manners; he was intellectual, he was clever, he wrote for the Press.

50 Next morning she had finished typing the article. She extinguished the gas-stove, restored the typewriter, loosed the catch of the outer door, banged the door after her, and descended, holding the foolscap envelope in her shabbily-gloved hand. The forsaken solitude of the office was behind her.

Along Clifford Street and all down Bond Street the heaped dustbins stood
55 on the kerb waiting for the scavengers. Nothing else moving in the thoroughfare! The Ritz Hotel, formidable fortress of luxury, stood up arrogant like a Florentine palace, hiding all its costly secrets from the scorned mob. No. 6a Jermyn Street was just round the corner from St James's Street: a narrow seven-storey building of flats, with a front-door as impressive and meaningless
60 as the face of a footman. Lilian hesitated a moment and relinquished her packet into the brass-bordered letter-slit. She turned away with a jerky gesture. She had not walked ten yards when a frightful lassitude and dejection attacked her with the suddenness of cholera. Scarcely could she command her limbs to move. The ineffable sadness, hopelessness, wretchedness, vanity of existence
65 washed over her and beat her down. Only a very few could be glorious, and she was not and never could be of the few. She was shut out from brightness—no better than a ragamuffin looking into a candy window.

She descended into the everlasting lamplit night of the Tube at Dover Street, where there was no dawn and no sunset. And all the employees, and all the
70 meek, preoccupied travellers seemed to be her brothers and sisters in martyrdom. Her train was nearly empty; but the eastbound trains—train after train —were full of pathetic midgets urgently engaged upon the problem of making both ends meet.

1 Lilian sits with 'a circle of radiance below' her (line 3) because
A her beauty illuminates everything around her
B moonlight falls through the window on to the floor
C her happiness seems to light up the room
D streetlamps throw their lights into the room
E the desk lamp casts its rays on to the desk top

2 For Lilian 'expensive flattery' (line 7) would probably take the form of
A lavish presents and compliments
B smart receptions and snobbishness
C gay parties and drink
D extravagant praise and adulation
E costly flowers and chocolates

3 That the man had been a 'vision' (line 18) implies that he
A had been in Lilian's dreams
B was from beyond the grave
C looked very handsome when young
D appeared only for a second
E used to be a famous actor

4 Lilian gives a 'prim counterfeit of a smile' (line 28) because
A she feels embarrassed after being asleep
B this is her professional welcome
C the man's appearance pleases her
D it is a relief to find her visitor friendly
E his uncertainty is rather amusing

5 Lilian falls asleep because she
A has nothing to do
B is alone and sad
C is tired-out
D has been day-dreaming
E is bored with her job

6 Lilian appears to be a
A copy typist
B secretary
C shorthand typist
D filing clerk
E receptionist

7 'spontaneously' (line 38) means

   A enthusiastically

   B pleasantly

   C involuntarily

   D gradually

   E eventually

8 The office *Who's Who* (lines 46–7) is

   A a telephone information service

   B the firm's clever busybody

   C Mr Grig, the agency owner

   D a reference book of the peerage

   E a directory of important people

9 'blood' (line 48) means

   A a love of hunting

   B high-ranking birth

   C a debauched life

   D ties of kinship

   E a passionate temperament

10 From 'the office *Who's Who*' Lilian could have discovered all the following about Lord Mackworth EXCEPT his

   A richness

   B peerage

   C demeanour

   D genealogy

   E journalism

11 The Ritz Hotel is referred to as a 'formidable fortress of luxury' (line 56) because it is

   I large and secure

   II impressive and dominating

   III reserved for army officers

   IV easily defended against mobs

   V occupied by powerful men

   A I and II only

   B I, II and V

   C I, III and V

   D II and IV only

   E II, IV and V

continue overleaf

12 The Ritz Hotel has all the following in common with a Florentine palace (lines 56–7) EXCEPT

   A many servants
   B rich clients
   C sumptuous food
   D beautiful rooms
   E lovely furniture

13 The 'costly secrets' (line 57) would most probably be

   A private expense accounts
   B hidden precious stones
   C lavish ways of life
   D anonymous visiting celebrities
   E disguised but heavy overcharging

14 The 'scorned mob' (line 57) is probably

   A angry crowds
   B rejected patrons
   C downtrodden tramps
   D ordinary people
   E superior groups

15 From lines 59–60 we gather that footmen's faces are

   A imperturbable but lacking intelligence
   B noble but lacking spirit
   C touching but lacking expression
   D exciting but lacking feeling
   E imposing but lacking significance

16 Lilian is suddenly attacked by 'lassitude and dejection' (line 62) when she becomes

   A tired of her gay private life
   B depressed by the early hour
   C aware of her social inferiority
   D disappointed at not seeing Lord Mackworth
   E gripped by a terrible disease

17 According to the passage cholera is a disease whose symptoms appear

   A instantaneously
   B imperceptibly
   C conspicuously
   D revoltingly
   E dishearteningly

18 Lilian feels 'no better than a ragamuffin looking into a candy window' (line 67), mainly because she is

   A wearing old torn clothes
   B desperately short of money
   C very fond of sweets
   D a humble working girl
   E in the cold street

19 The 'martyrdom' which Lilian shares with her fellow travellers (lines 70–1) consists of

   A travelling by Tube
   B being working-class
   C having to daydream
   D living in London
   E feeling perpetually exhausted

20 The eastbound travellers are 'pathetic midgets' (line 72) in Lilian's eyes because they are

   A pitiable puppets of the rich
   B terribly crushed during the journey
   C obnoxious insect-like creatures
   D distressingly deformed in body
   E undersized people for special jobs

Passage Two

The city water pipes in Rome were usually of baked clay or lead; copper was sometimes used and also hollowed stone. For the large supply conduits leading to the city the Romans used covered channels with free water surfaces, rather than pipes. Perhaps this choice was a matter of economics, for apparently
5 they could make lead pipes up to 15 inches in diameter. While pipes can follow the profile of undulating ground, with the pressure increasing in the lower areas, channels cannot. They must slope continuously downwards, because water in channels does not normally flow uphill; and the grade must be flat, from 1 in 60 in small channels to perhaps 1 in 3,000 in large ones, to keep the
10 water speed down to a few feet per second. Thus the main supply channels or aqueducts had long lengths of flat grade and where they crossed depressions or valleys they were carried on elevated stone bridges in the form of tiered arches. At the beginning of the Christian era there were over 30 miles of these raised aqueducts in the 250 miles of channels and tunnels bringing water to
15 Rome. The channels were up to 6 feet wide and 5 to 8 feet high. Sometimes channels were later added on the tops of existing ones. The remains of some of these aqueducts still grace the skyline on the outskirts of Rome and elsewhere in Europe similar ruins are found.

Brick and stone drains were constructed in various parts of Rome. The
20 oldest existing one is the Cloaca Maxima which follows the course of an old stream. It dates back at least to the third century B.C. Later the drains were used for sewage, flushed by water from the public baths and fountains, as well as street storm run-off.

The truly surprising aspect of the achievements of all the ancient hydraulic
25 artisans is the lack of theoretical knowledge behind their designs. Apart from the hydrostatics of Archimedes, there was no sound understanding of the most elementary principles of fluid behaviour. Sextus Frontinus, Rome's water commissioner around A.D. 100, did not fully realize that in order to calculate the volume rate of flow in a channel it is necessary to allow for the
30 speed of the flow as well as the area of cross-section. The Romans' flow standard was the rate at which water would flow through a bronze pipe roughly $\frac{3}{4}$ inch in diameter and 9 inches long. When this pipe was connected to the side of a water-supply pipe or channel as a delivery outlet, it was assumed that the outflow was at the standard rate. In fact, the amount of
35 water delivered depended not only on the cross-sectional area of the outlet pipe but also on the speed of water flowing through it and this speed depended on the pressure in the supply pipe.

Vitruvius, however, a Roman engineer of the first century A.D., was the first to state, correctly, that ground water is mostly derived from rain and snow by infiltration from the ground surface. He also proposed a design for a water-driven wheel for grinding corn. An earlier type known as the Greek or Norse mill, which had a series of water vanes fixed to a vertical spindle, had been in use possibly for centuries in the rapidly flowing rivers of northern Italy. The Vitruvian model had a vertical paddle wheel whose lower part dipped into the stream. The horizontal axle was connected through a wooden reduction gear to the millstone. In this way a wheel 7 feet in diameter could grind 400 lb of corn an hour, corresponding to the output of a 3-horse-power motor. By the fourth century the Romans had quite large installations in several parts of Europe. One 16-wheel unit near Arles in France handled 3 tons of corn an hour, sufficient for a population of 80,000.

1 The Romans used all of the following to make water pipes EXCEPT

A earth

B wood

C copper

D lead

E stone

2 Covered channels were used instead of pipes to supply large quantities of water probably because

A the Romans could produce them more cheaply

B they could follow uneven ground more easily

C the Romans could not build large pipes

D they avoided rapid changes of pressure

E they could be made to flow continuously downhill

3 Compared with smaller water channels larger ones need to be

A laid quite flat

B made much shallower

C inclined less steeply

D carried on arches

E led across valleys

4 'aqueducts' (line 11) are essentially

A stone bridges

B water courses

C copper conduits

D clay tunnels

E tiered arches

5 The use of 'grace' in line 17 suggests that the aqueducts today are

A hideous

B divine

C useful

D attractive

E interesting

6 From its immediate context and your knowledge of English words, which of the following do you think is the best translation of 'Cloaca Maxima' (line 20)?

A the biggest sewer

B the highest aqueduct

C the oldest stream

D the deepest river

E the best drain

7 The Romans, it is suggested, could not construct
  A large metal pipes
  B proper drainage sewers
  C attractive water fountains
  D accurate water gauges
  E powerful water wheels

8 It is astounding that ancient water designers and engineers
  A could not make good drains
  B had only practical knowledge
  C did not have adequate pumps
  D were basically poor artisans
  E built only enormous aqueducts

9 'hydrostatics' (line 26) is essentially the science which investigates liquids and their
  A early scientific histories
  B use in baths and drains
  C volumes and pressures
  D influence on stationary bodies
  E effect on man's development

10 In order to calculate accurately the volume of water flowing through a pipe it is important to know its speed AND

  I the area across the end of the pipe
  II the length of the pipe
  III the water pressure in the pipe
  IV the level from which the water falls

  A I and II only
  B I and III only
  C II and III only
  D II and IV only
  E III and IV only

11 The Romans' standard measurement of the flow of water was basically unsatisfactory because it failed to take into consideration the
  A speed of the water
  B pressure of the water
  C quantity of the water
  D cross-section of the pipe
  E length of the pipe

continue overleaf

12 The first to have any completely sound theoretical knowledge of the behaviour of water was

A Archimedes
B Sextus Frontinus
C Vitruvius
D the Italians
E the Norse

13 Vitruvius's major contribution to theoretical science was the correct explanation of the

A source of river water
B origin of rain water
C invention of the water-wheel
D mechanical grinding of corn
E use of horizontal spindles

14 'infiltration' (line 40) means

A fissuring
B evaporation
C absorption
D flooding
E erosion

15 Vitruvius's proposed water-wheel differed from Greek mill-wheels because it

A could be used in fast rivers
B did not use much water
C revolved like a gramophone record
D made use of water vanes
E turned like the wheel of a car

16 In relation to the water-wheel a 'reduction gear' (line 46) made the mill-stones turn

A more smoothly
B more accurately
C at the same speed
D more slowly
E more quickly

17 The passage suggests that the skill of the Romans lay mainly in

A farm-irrigation
B theoretical science
C civil engineering
D wheel-making
E corn-milling

18 The Romans used their knowledge of the behaviour of water for all the following aspects of their civilization EXCEPT

- **A** common sewers
- **B** municipal fountains
- **C** corn-mills
- **D** underfloor-heating
- **E** public baths

19 The main subject of the whole passage is concerned essentially with

- **A** classical scientific achievements
- **B** theoretical Greek hydrostatics
- **C** ancient Roman hydrology
- **D** early European engineering
- **E** primitive methods of corn-grinding

20 The fundamental style of the passage can best be described as

- **A** figurative
- **B** explanatory
- **C** elaborate
- **D** philosophical
- **E** meditative

TEST 6

Answer all questions. Do not guess.

Passage One

It was on a Friday afternoon when Annette decided to leave the Ringenhall Ladies' College.

I am learning nothing here, she thought. From now on I shall educate myself. I shall enter the School of Life.

5   Annette was nearly nineteen. Concerning Ringenhall she herself had not experienced a single moment of doubt. She had loathed it from the very first day. For the headmistress, a Miss Walpole, she felt a pure and disinterested hatred. Miss Walpole had never behaved unpleasantly to Annette or indeed paid any attention to her whatsoever. Annette had never hated anyone in this
10 way before and took pride in the emotion,which she felt to be a sign of maturity. Against the Ringenhall curriculum she had fought with unremitting obstinacy, determined not to let a single one of the ideas which it purveyed find even a temporary lodgement in her mind.

There was one thing which Annette had wanted very much to do ever since
15 she had arrived, which was to swing on the chandelier in the dining-room. She turned rapidly in the direction of that room and bounded in. Tables and chairs stood by, silent with disapproval. Annette looked up at the chandelier which hung from a stout chain and had a very strong metal bar, right in the centre of it. All about and above this bar were suspended tiny drops of crystal,
20 each one glowing with a drop of pure light tinier still, as if a beautiful wave had been arrested in the act of breaking while the sun was shining upon it. Annette had felt sure that if she could swing upon the chandelier the music which was hidden in the crystals would break out into a great peal of bells.

Grimly she began to pull one of the chairs into the centre. By standing on
25 tiptoe on it she could get her hands over the metal bar. She paused breathlessly. Then with a quick movement she kicked the chair away and hung stiffly in mid-air.

With an oscillation from the hips she began to swing very gently to and fro. The chandelier began to ring, not with a deafening peal but with a very high
30 and sweet tinkling sound; the sort of sound, after all, which you would expect a wave of the sea to make if it had been immobilized and turned into glass: a tiny internal rippling, a mixture of sound and light.

At that moment the door opened and Miss Walpole came in. Annette, who was at the end of one of her swings, let go abruptly of the chandelier
35 and, missing the table, fell to the floor with a crash at Miss Walpole's feet. Miss Walpole looked down at her with a slight frown.

'Get up, Miss Cockeyne', she said to Annette in her usual weary tone of voice.

As she never cared particularly about anything, so nothing much ever
40 surprised her. This calm indifference had won her the reputation of being a
good headmistress.

Annette got up, rubbing herself.

'What were you doing, Miss Cockeyne?' asked Miss Walpole, sighing.

'Swinging from the chandelier', said Annette. She was not afraid of her
45 headmistress, whose claims to moral or intellectual excellence she had seen
through some time ago.

'Why?' asked Miss Walpole.

Annette had no ready answer to this, and thought she might as well skip
a point or two in the conversation by saying immediately, 'I'm sorry.' Then she
50 said 'I've decided to leave Ringenhall.'

'May I again ask why?' asked Miss Walpole.

She was an extremely tall woman, which was also perhaps one of the secrets
of her success, and although Annette, too, was tall, she had to throw her head
back if she wanted to look into Miss Walpole's eyes. Annette took a step or
55 two away and receded until the line which joined her eyes to Miss Walpole's
made a nearer approach to the horizontal. She wanted to look dignified. But
as she moved away, Miss Walpole imperceptibly approached, gliding forward
as if propelled from behind, so that Annette had once more to crane her neck.

'I have learnt all that I can learn here', said Annette. 'From now on I shall
60 educate myself. I shall go out into the School of Life.'

'As for the institution which you call the School of Life,' said Miss Walpole,
'I doubt, if I may venture a personal opinion, whether you are yet qualified
to benefit from its curriculum.'

1 'Annette decided to leave the Ringenhall Ladies' College' (lines 1–2) because she
  A was well past the school-leaving age
  B realized that her expulsion was imminent
  C had gained entry to a much better school
  D did not enjoy good relations with her Head
  E considered her instruction to be quite worthless

2 'the School of Life' (line 4) is
  A education through experience
  B a famous art college
  C lessons by correspondence
  D a health clinic
  E an institute of biography

3 From her first day at Ringenhall Annette's main feelings for the school have been
  A justifiable anger
  B desultory affection
  C eccentric interest
  D constant aversion
  E unfair amusement

4 'disinterested hatred' (lines 7–8) is extreme dislike which is
  A kept up with increasing force
  B not influenced by private feelings
  C wearisome and boring to maintain
  D ever decreasing in its intensity
  E felt throughout one's whole life

5 Annette is pleased with her feelings towards Miss Walpole as they
  A seemed the way adults experienced things
  B made her look much more sophisticated
  C helped to change the whole school timetable
  D gave her status among her schoolfriends
  E repaid the Headmistress for her indifference

6 The 'curriculum' (line 11) is the school's
  A Board of Governors
  B sixth-form society
  C religious instruction lessons
  D course of study
  E Head and Staff

7 Annette is 'determined' (line 12) not to

  A bother about the Head's opinion of her

  B worry about her popularity with her classmates

  C learn or remember anything from her school

  D care if the school governors expelled her

  E accept her prizes at the end of term

8 The dining-room tables and chairs are said to be 'silent with disapproval' (line 17) mainly because

  A the cook had arranged the room like a court

  B special polish prevented the furniture from creaking

  C the dining-room staff were ruining the equipment

  D Annette felt guilty about what she intended to do

  E the furniture was not to be disturbed after lunch

9 Annette considered that the chandelier would bear her weight because it

   I was suspended by a series of powerful links

  II had been made of specially toughened glass

 III copied the construction of a mighty ocean wave

 IV possessed a sturdy rod running across its middle

  V held the strength of a great peal of bells

  A I and II only

  B I and IV only

  C II and IV only

  D II and V only

  E III and V only

10 The chandelier is said to resemble a wave 'arrested in the act of breaking while the sun was shining upon it' (lines 20–1) because it is all the following EXCEPT

  A glittering

  B made up of globules

  C delicately strong

  D pretty

  E curved up to a crest

11 'the music which was hidden in the crystals' (lines 22–3) would be released by their

  A having strong light shone into them

  B being placed in large belfries

  C striking haphazardly against one another

  D hangings knocking against each other

  E being dragged through pure sea water

continue overleaf

12 As well as containing a drop of light, each crystal is said to contain

A glass beads

B water globules

C magic power

D latent melodies

E metal clappers

13 In order to make the chandelier swing we are told that Annette has to do all the following EXCEPT

A consider the main problems

B climb on a chair

C grasp the central bar

D move with a regular pace

E dangle without movement

14 Between the appearance of the chandelier's crystals and the noise they make when swinging there is

A exact correlation

B approximate likeness

C partial resemblance

D little correspondence

E no similarity

15 A major reason for Miss Walpole's success as a Headmistress is that she

A never appears to be taken unawares

B was always catching out her pupils

C usually had a sternly forbidding look

D rarely seemed to be very approachable

E normally spoke in a bored tone

16 Miss Walpole's 'claims to moral or intellectual excellence' (line 45) implies that she

A seeks the highest rewards for school and herself

B demands the best standards in ethics and schoolwork

C uses university qualifications she has not been awarded

D pretends to be spiritually perfect

E alleges that she is the cleverest teacher

17 Annette steps back from Miss Walpole (lines 54–5) in order to

A escape from her angry gaze

B tell her that she is leaving

C snap the thread joining them

D look her comfortably in the eye

E make herself seem equally tall

18 Miss Walpole's main way of dominating her pupils is to

   A move with grace

   B use her height

   C look very threatening

   D drive them backwards

   E tie them up

19 Miss Walpole's reaction to Annette's announcement that she is to enter the School of Life is to be

   A indifferent

   B disappointed

   C understanding

   D amused

   E sarcastic

20 Annette's character could be described by all the following words EXCEPT

   A determined

   B athletic

   C uneducated

   D daring

   E fearless

Passage Two
The chemist's shop sells aspirins and dispenses penicillin prescriptions. The child's chemistry set makes colours, smells, and bangs. In fact, the essence of chemistry consists of the making of new substances, and a chemical change is defined as the changing of one substance into another. Many such chemical
5 changes have been performed by man since very early times, probably the earliest being the heating of clay to make pottery, which has been known for 10,000 years. Even before this, of course, man had discovered fire—another chemical change—but here the importance of the reaction lies in the heat-energy produced rather than in the ashes, smoke, and gases which are
10 the final products.

Progress in chemistry was slow because of the absence of any adequate theory to explain these changes, and because the earliest theory ('alchemy') was so blindly optimistic as to assume that anything could be changed into anything else. In particular, the alchemists thought that they could change
15 a cheap metal like lead into gold and so get rich quickly. Not until less than 200 years ago were the true foundations of chemistry laid by painstaking researches into the nature of air and water, in fact by pure disinterested curiosity, allied to the habit of mind which takes nothing for granted. Chemists learned that before they could make new substances they must first discover
20 what ordinary things are made of; in technical language, analysis must always precede synthesis.

Chemistry is closely related to physics, and the dividing line between them is by no means a sharp one. The revolutionary discoveries in physics at the end of the nineteenth century—X-rays, radioactivity, and the electron—
25 enormously speeded up chemical discoveries, and completely altered our ideas of the unchanging and unchangeable atoms which had done such good service for nearly 100 years. Now the atomic piles have produced new kinds of atoms which were hitherto unavailable to the chemist, plutonium being the most spectacular example, and 'labelled atoms' (artificially radioactive) which
30 enable the chemist to follow the progress of chemical changes by observing where the radioactivity has got to. On a humbler but more immediately useful level, electricity will cause chemical change to occur, such as the production of aluminium or the charging of an accumulator, and chemical changes such as the discharge of an accumulator will produce electricity.
35 The relationship of chemistry to biology is no less close. Nearly all the activities of living matter are caused by chemical changes, many of them of great complexity and by no means yet fully understood. The most fundamental activity, that of respiration, is the chemical combination of foodstuffs with

74

the oxygen of the air in order to produce the energy needed for all the other
40 bodily processes. Chemical substances may profoundly alter the normal
reactions of the body in many ways: analgesics reduce sensitivity and so
lessen pain; local and general anaesthetics do this on a progressively greater
scale; extra supplies of substances needed normally may be helpful, such as
vitamins, proteins, fluorides, hormones.

45 The largest field of all for chemical discovery is, however, the production
of new materials for our everyday needs. New sources of power have been
discovered for coal gas, explosives of all kinds, and fuel oils—especially for
cars and aeroplanes. Age-old processes like the manufacture of glass and of
metals have been transformed and new substances made, such as Pyrex,
50 stainless steel, and light alloys, which do not break or rust so easily as the
old. New sources of food have been tapped, with margarine made from
otherwise inedible oils, sugar from beet, and large increases in agricultural
yields through the application of fertilizers. The clothing revolution is only
half complete, but rayon, ardil, nylon, and terylene, coupled with water-
55 softeners, detergents, and cheap dyestuffs have already made life much more
cheerful. Finally, the plastics are new materials which give rise to hitherto
unthought-of uses; their forerunner, rubber, almost deserves a history to
itself with its applications to waterproofs, car tyres, hose-pipes, and hot-water
bottles; but celluloid (and hence popular photography and the cinema),
60 bakelite, PVC, polythene, perspex, silicones, and many others are even wider
in their scope.

Chemistry, therefore, is the conquest of materials, the making of new
substances which are useful either in themselves or for the control of living
material.

1 The first chemical change discovered by man was probably

   A clay

   B pottery

   C fire

   D heat-energy

   E gas

2 The earliest chemical change noticed by man interested him primarily because

   A it marked the beginning of chemistry

   B he was keen to make pottery

   C it provided a source of energy

   D its by-products were valuable

   E clay had been difficult to handle

3 The advance of chemistry was initially delayed by all of the following EXCEPT

   A early beliefs in alchemy

   B very detailed investigations

   C optimistic research studies

   D theories on the interchangeability of matter

   E the search for the manufacture of precious metal

4 Continued progress in chemistry became possible only when scientists

   A produced theories to explain chemical changes

   B attempted to change lead into gold

   C experimented to increase their wealth

   D examined the nature of air and water

   E learned to be objective and curious

5 Before chemists could make new substances they were first obliged to

   A discover the composition of common substances

   B invent technical terms for their earlier discoveries

   C synthesize all the information available to them

   D examine the difference between chemistry and physics

   E understand all the work of earlier scientists

6 In its immediate context 'synthesis' (line 21) means

   A disinterested curiosity

   B painstaking research

   C the examination of existing substances

   D the discovery of new materials

   E the use of technical language

7 Physics helped the progress of chemistry by all the following EXCEPT
   A accelerating greatly the rate of chemical discoveries
   B revising earlier theories about the nature of matter
   C discovering X-rays, radioactivity, and the electron
   D showing that the atom was unchanging and unchangeable
   E pointing the way to the discovery of new atoms

8 'labelled atoms' (line 29) are used principally in
   A making other atoms artificially radioactive
   B analysing detailed atomic reactions
   C tracing the development of chemical changes
   D discovering new chemical classifications
   E measuring heat-energy in atomic piles

9 All of the following statements can be deduced from the passage EXCEPT
   A chemical changes can be caused by electricity
   B chemical changes can produce electricity
   C chemical changes can make an accumulator discharge
   D aluminium is used in the production of electricity
   E electricity is used in the production of aluminium

10 The relationship of chemistry to biology is described as 'close' (line 35) because both sciences are concerned with
   A chemical changes
   B living matter
   C complex experiments
   D unexplained phenomena
   E fundamental activities

11 Which of the following are not normally required for healthy bodily activity?
   A proteins
   B hormones
   C analgesics
   D vitamins
   E fluorides

12 A 'local' anaesthetic (line 42) is one that
   A makes the patient lose consciousness
   B makes foreign substances in the body inactive
   C is used only for minor dental operations
   D makes only part of the body insensitive to pain
   E is normally administered by the nearest hospital

continue overleaf

13 'progressively' (line 42) means

A increasingly

B markedly

C correspondingly

D demonstrably

E comparatively

14 The greatest scope for the chemist to make new discoveries lies in the field of

A atomic and nuclear physics

B radioactive materials

C substances for our daily lives

D sources of power and energy

E biological and medical science

15 The writer does not suggest in the passage that the chemist has

A improved the durability of goods

B reduced the cost of living

C made life happier

D provided new sources of power

E increased food production

16 Which of the following is not a synthetic material discovered by the chemist?

A coal gas

B stainless steel

C margarine

D rayon

E detergent

17 The writer does not suggest that the 'clothing revolution' (line 53) has depended on

A nylon

B detergents

C dyes

D fashion

E water-softeners

18 The passage argues that chemistry and the physical sciences are

A independent

B interdependent

C equally important

D easily differentiated

E identical

19 The primary purpose of chemistry is to produce
   A better medicines and drugs for mankind
   B more interesting and varied colours
   C substantially newer smells and bangs
   D materials that have not existed before
   E useful synthetic materials for our daily lives

20 The chemist has significantly improved all of the following EXCEPT our
   A entertainment
   B health
   C morality
   D nourishment
   E transport

TEST 7

Answer all questions. Do not guess.

Passage One

[Some years after Lettie had married Leslie instead of George, George came down to London and consented to stay with the narrator.]

    I wrote and told him that Lettie and Leslie too were in London, and that we should dine with them one evening. I met him at King's Cross and we drove
5 west. We left the car at the Marble Arch corner and listened to a little speaker who was flaring fiercely under a plane tree. The hot stream of his words flowed over the old wounds that the knowledge of the unending miseries of the poor had given me, and I winced. For him the world was all East End, and all the East End was as a pool from which the waters are drained off, leaving
10 the water-things to wrestle in the wet mud under the sun, till the whole of the city seems a heaving, shuddering struggle of black-mudded objects deprived of the elements of life. I felt a greater terror of the little man, lest he should make me see all mud, as I had seen before. Then I felt a breathless pity for him, that his eyes should be always filled with mud, and never brightened. George
15 listened intently to the speaker, very much moved by him.

    At night, we saw the outcasts sleep in a rank under the Waterloo Bridge, their heads to the wall, their feet lying out on the pavement: a long, black, ruffled heap at the foot of the wall. All the faces were covered but two, that of a peaked, pale little man, and that of a brutal woman. Over these two faces,
20 floating like uneasy pale dreams on their obscurity, swept now and again the trailing light of the tram cars. We picked our way past the line of abandoned feet, shrinking from the sight of the thin ankles of a young man, from the draggled edge of the skirts of a bunched-up woman, from the pitiable sight of the men who had wrapped their legs in newspaper for a little warmth, and
25 lay like worthless parcels. It was raining.

    I had accepted the early invitation of Lettie and Leslie who were staying up at Hampstead with a friend of the Tempests.

    George was exceedingly quiet when we visited them. He spoke a few words now and then but on the whole he was altogether silent, listening.
30   'Really!' Lettie was saying, 'I don't see that one thing is worth doing any more than another. It's like dessert: you are equally indifferent whether you have grapes, or pears, or pineapple. The only thing worth doing is producing. That is the only thing one finds any pleasure in—that is to say, any satisfaction. Do you not think so?' she added.
35   'Do you write poetry then?' asked George.

    'I! Oh, dear no! I have tried strenuously to make up a limerick for a competition, but in vain. So you see, I am a failure there. Did you know I have a son, though?—a marvellous little fellow, is he not, Leslie?—he is my work. I am a wonderful mother, am I not, Leslie?'

40   'Too devoted', Leslie replied.

'There!' she exclaimed in triumph—'When I have to sign my name and occupation in a visitor's book, it will be '—— Mother.' I hope my business will flourish', she concluded, smiling.

George looked and listened to all the flutter of conversation, and said
45   nothing. It seemed to him like so much unreasonable rustling of pieces of paper, of leaves of books, and so on.

We left before eleven.

When we were seated in the cab and rushing down hill, he said:

'You know, she makes me mad.'

50   He was frowning, looking out of the window away from me.

'Who, Lettie? Why, what riles you?' I asked.

He was some time in replying.

'She's so affected.'

We got out at Victoria. In the vast cavern of the station the theatre-goers
55   were hastening, crossing the pale grey strand, small creatures scurrying hither and thither in the space beneath the lonely lamps. As the train crawled over the river we watched the far-flung hoop of diamond lights curving slowly round and striping with bright threads the black water. He sat looking with heavy eyes, seeming to shrink from the enormous unintelligible lettering of
60   the poem of London.

The town was too large for him, he could not take in its immense, its stupendous poetry. What did come home to him was its flagrant discords. The unintelligibility of the vast city made him apprehensive, and the crudity of its big, coarse contrasts wounded him unutterably.

1 To judge from the passage, the area by Marble Arch is known as

   A the East End

   B Speakers' Corner

   C the World's End

   D Hackney Marshes

   E the Pool of London

2 The little speaker is probably said to be 'flaring' (line 5) because he is

   A dazzling everyone with his oratory

   B shouting coarse offensive insults

   C speaking with occasional loud outbursts

   D standing in flickering torch light

   E wearing his traditional Cockney clothes

3 The effect of the speaker's harangue on the narrator is compared with the

   A washing of unhealed gashes

   B soothing of deep bruises

   C sterilizing of sore gashes

   D scouring of broken skin

   E scalding of past injuries

4 'the world was all East End' (line 8) implies that the speaker thinks

   A everywhere is utterly degraded

   B only of the East End of London

   C everything worthwhile is oriental

   D the East End is the best

   E everyone admires the Cockneys

5 Lines 9–13 of the passage compare life in London with the

   A degrading events in a wrestling ring

   B unspeakable horror of a slimy snake-pit

   C terrible consequences of an Easter flood

   D immediate results of emptying a pond

   E unpleasant situation on a hot oily beach

6 The best explanation of the phrase 'deprived of the elements of life' (lines 11–12) is

   A bereaved by the terrible loss of their fellow-creatures

   B cut off from the basic conditions for existence

   C robbed of all the nicest things under the sun

   D dispossessed of their traditional warm breeding ground

   E removed from the many pleasures of the flesh

7 The narrator feels 'pity' (line 13) for the speaker because his
  A views are so depressed and distorted
  B face is so dirt and filth spattered
  C ideas are so foul and wicked
  D eyes are so clouded and diseased
  E mind is so dull and drink sodden

8 'peaked' (line 19) means
  A with pointed features
  B thin and sickly
  C wearing a cap
  D old and spent
  E sporting a quiff

9 The dreams of the man and woman and the light of the tramcars (lines 20–1) are said to be

   I wan
  II intermittent
 III protracted
  IV drifting
   V vivid

  A I, II and IV only
  B I, III and V only
  C II, III and V only
  D II, IV and V only
  E III, IV and V only

10 The people sleeping under the bridge seem to be all the following EXCEPT
  A poor vagabonds
  B completely covered
  C in a row
  D on the sidewalk
  E feet to the street

11 'obscurity' (line 20) is a state of living in
  A nauseating filth
  B hopeless confusion
  C secluded darkness
  D financial difficulties
  E foolish delusion

continue overleaf

12 The author makes a comparison between sleeping men and worthless parcels (lines 24–5) because they both appear to be

  I tied with string
  II covered with paper
  III contain valueless objects
  IV insensible to feeling
  V resting quite inertly

  A I, II and III only
  B I, IV and V only
  C II, III and V only
  D II, IV and V only
  E III, IV and V only

13 Lettie appears to believe that the pre-eminent thing in life is to
  A eat
  B talk
  C tease
  D create
  E please

14 All 'desserts' (line 31) are
  A separations of married couples
  B barren wastes of sand
  C rich and exotic fruits
  D sweet courses of meals
  E just punishments for wrong-doing

15 Lettie's creative ability mainly takes the form of
  A writing poems
  B devising recipes
  C giving autographs
  D making money
  E being maternal

16 A 'limerick' (line 36) is a poem which is
  A only about Ireland
  B short and humorous
  C only for contests
  D long and serious
  E only for amateurs

17 To George the conversation at Hampstead seems like the rustling of leaves of books (lines 45–6) because it is

A meaningless
B crisp
C literary
D inflammatory
E murmured

18 The lights are said to be striping the water (line 58) with their

A straightness
B shadows
C fluctuations
D narrowness
E reflections

19 'flagrant discords' (line 62) is best replaced by

A glaring differences
B jarring noises
C harsh quarrels
D scandalous feuds
E obvious unfairness

20 During his visit to London George visits all the following places EXCEPT

A Marble Arch
B the East End
C Waterloo Bridge
D the Tempests' home
E Victoria Station

Passage Two

Although it must have been seen for centuries that the distant scene in landscape appears to become more and more blue the farther it is away, Leonardo da Vinci seems to have been the first to try to analyse the phenomenon. In his notebooks he suggests that it must be due to moisture in the atmosphere. He
5 also notes how the smoke of a bonfire appears blue under certain conditions of light, and supposes that these atmospheric blues are related to the blue of the sky.

It was John Tyndall, the physicist, who first accurately explained the phenomenon in the mid-nineteenth century, and it is now named after him—
10 Tyndall's effect. The blue sky is filled with motes and tiny globules of moisture. These are comparable in dimension to the shorter wave-lengths of the visible spectrum, the blue-violet end. The longer waves of red and yellow pass through this filter of particles; the blue-violet waves are scattered and reflected. The intensity of the blue depends upon the size and density of the packing
15 of the particles.

The intense blue of the wings of Brazilian butterflies is a similar blue. Here it is the tiny scales and configurations on the upper surface of the wing that reflect the blue light. The blueness is increased by the actual pigmentation of the wing, which is a dark warm brown. This deeper layer absorbs all the
20 yellow-red light so that none is reflected to interfere with the blue. This brown is the only pigment on the wing, as can be clearly seen if the wing is held against the light. Then all the blue colour seems to evaporate from it and it becomes a gauzy brown membrane. This *structural* blue colour, so called because it depends on light alone and not on pigment, is found everywhere in
25 nature, in the jay's wing and the pigeon's breast, in the green of a mallard's head or the iridescent peacock's tail, and in many fish and reptiles too.

Any emulsion of fine particles suspended in a fluid medium will produce a similar result. If we spill milk upon a mahogany table, the milky smear looks blue. Milk is an emulsion, a mixture of tiny particles of fat suspended in water.
30 Paint is another such mixture of tiny particles of pigment in some sort of fluid medium, such as linseed oil. If the pigment is opaque then its grains will scatter blue light and the paint will turn blue optically. This blueness will be quite independent of pigmentary colour or colour mixtures, but obviously will be more apparent in lighter colours, that is to say colours with a fair
35 amount of white in their composition. This includes, of course, the whole range of flesh colours, and this is where the effect is most valuable.

The painter of a portrait starts with his prepared ground on panel or canvas. This is basically dense and light reflecting, usually white. On this

ground he draws his subject in very thin red-brown paint, using it rather like
40 a wash or ink. The tones follow the final modelling but are much exaggerated.
The shadows are very dark and are carried well over into the lighter parts
of the composition. When this layer of paint is dry, the next is laid on. This
is a ready-mixed pale yellowy-pink flesh tint with plenty of white body to it
and just enough oil and turpentine to make it workable. The pink, warm
45 flesh tone is applied quite densely in the lighter parts of the head, on the brow
or cheek for example. This layer is smeared out over the brown underpainting
into the shaded half-tone areas, perhaps with a brush, but quite often with the
ball of the thumb or side of the hand. When this attenuated layer becomes
a thin film over the underpainted shadow, it takes on a cold, bluish hue like
50 the spilt milk on the table. The brown underpainting absorbs the yellow-red
light wavelengths and stops them from reflecting back, while the pigment
particles in the top layer scatter and reflect the blue. The darkest shadows are
left alone, as first painted. Finally detail such as cold white highlights are
painted in, and fine lines added to represent hair, eyelashes, eye pupils, lips,
55 braids, and so on. These were sometimes painted in tempera, a mixture of
oil and egg yolk which, like mayonnaise, permits the addition of water in
order to thin it down.

Having made his observations on the behaviour of light and atmosphere
in landscape, Leonardo, however, never applied his knowledge to the painting
60 of landscape itself.

1 Leonardo da Vinci offered as an explanation of the blueness in landscape
  A the influence of the sky
  B the presence of water droplets
  C a trick of the light
  D its contamination by bonfire smoke
  E its relative distance away

2 The explanation offered by Leonardo of the 'phenomenon' set out in the first paragraph was not the first
  A analysis based on observation
  B description by a painter
  C scientifically accurate account
  D to appear in a notebook
  E to associate it with the sky

3 'Tyndall's effect' (line 10) was first noticed by
  A pre-fifteenth-century men
  B Leonardo da Vinci
  C observant ornithologists
  D Brazilian naturalists
  E a mid-nineteenth-century scientist

4 The 'motes' referred to in line 10 are
  A small flies
  B tiny insects
  C light beams
  D dust specks
  E cloud formations

5 'spectrum' (line 12) means
  A a range of light waves
  B a large, natural rainbow
  C a broad expanse of sky
  D a freak distortion of light
  E a pattern of light and dark

6 When blue light waves meet atmospheric obstructions of the kind mentioned in 'Tyndall's effect' they are
  A filtered
  B destroyed
  C not affected
  D not absorbed
  E not reflected

7 The wings of the Brazilian butterfly appear very blue because they have

   I   surfaces that can reflect light
   II scales covering the whole surface
   III a warm, dark blue pigmentation
   IV a warm, dark brown pigmentation

   A I and II only
   B I and III only
   C II and III only
   D II and IV only
   E III and IV only

8 When the wings of the Brazilian butterfly are held up to the light they
   A become transparent
   B are translucent
   C seem to vanish
   D slowly disintegrate
   E look very rough

9 '*structural*' (line 23) is in italics because the
   A word is used wrongly
   B word does not really mean 'structural'
   C same blue appears elsewhere in nature
   D butterfly's wings are not really blue
   E writer is quoting from Tyndall's work

10 The jay's wing appears blue in places because it
   A has a blue pigmentation
   B can change its natural colour
   C absorbs blue light from the sky
   D absorbs red band light
   E resembles a pigeon's breast

11 The phenomenon known as 'Tyndall's effect' cannot be observed in the colours of
   A bonfire smoke
   B a mallard's head
   C a peacock's tail
   D a jay's wing
   E a mahogany table

continue overleaf

12 'iridescent' (line 26) means
  A deep blue
  B structurally blue
  C greenish blue
  D rainbow-coloured
  E brightly luminous

13 'optically' (line 32) means
  A under a microscope
  B through spectacles
  C as an alternative
  D in the viewer's sight
  E slowly and gradually

14 The word 'obviously' (line 33) is used to suggest that lighter colours contain a greater proportion of pigments which are
  A thickly granular
  B not blue
  C not transparent
  D quite independent
  E in solution

15 'ground' (line 37) is used technically to mean
  A underlying colour
  B outlined landscape
  C fine canvas
  D background details
  E coloured sketch

16 The passage suggests a portrait painter initially makes use of white paint because it is
  A opaque and returns some light rays
  B light-absorbent and flattering to the skin
  C flesh-coloured and helps to give reality
  D independent of pigmentary colour and light
  E a contrast to ink and red-brown paint

17 The shadows produced by the thin red-brown paint are carried over into the lighter parts of the painting primarily in order to
  A absorb all yellow-red light
  B reduce the effect of reflected blue light
  C produce definite and pronounced highlights
  D sketch in the final modelling
  E exaggerate the portrait's features

18 The painter adds yellowy-pink flesh-coloured paint to underpainted red-brown areas to produce a colour which looks

A whitish
B yellowish
C pinkish
D bluish
E brownish

19 'attenuated' (line 48) means

A spread out]
B finished off
C indistinct
D smudged
E emulsified

20 The passage explicitly suggests that tempera and mayonnaise are similar in all of the following respects EXCEPT

A both contain eggs
B both are yellow
C both are made with oil
D both can be thinned
E both can be watered down

Answer all questions. Do not guess.

Passage One

In the bookshop of Violet and Henry, Elsie, the maid, it always was who every morning breathed the breath of life into the dead nocturnal house, and revived it, and turned it once again from a dark, unresponsive, meaningless and death-like keep into a human habitation. The dawn helped, but Elsie was the chief
5 agent.

A beautiful October morning, thought Elsie as she naughtily lingered for ten seconds at the window instead of getting on with her job. She enjoyed the fresh chill air blowing through Riceyman Steps. Conscience pricked her; she shut the window. Taking crockery and cutlery from the interior of the side-
10 board, she rapidly laid breakfast for two. The parlour was now humanized, despite the unlit fire. With a glance at the clock, which rivalled Greenwich in exactitude, but which had a mysterious and disconcerting habit of hurrying when she wanted it to loiter, Elsie hastened away to the bathroom and gave a knock on the bedroom door as she passed. The bathroom was beautifully
15 warm. She rolled up her tight sleeves, put on a rough apron, and pushed the oval tub under the thin trickle of steaming water that issued from the burning geyser. She was absorbed utterly in her great life-work, and in the problem of fitting the various parts of it into spaces of time which would scarcely hold them. She had the true devotee's conviction that something very grave, some-
20 thing disastrously affecting the whole world, would happen if she fell short of her ideal in labour. As she bent over the linen in the tub she hummed 'God Save the King' to herself.

Violet went down into the shop just after the first-post delivery and just before Henry came. She noticed the accumulation of dirt in the shop, very
25 gradual, but resistless. In Henry's eyes, however, the shop was clean and he was content with it; he deprecated his wife's lamentations about its condition. Certainly no one could deny that it still was cleaner than before her advent, and anyhow he could never again have tolerated vacuum-cleaning, with its absurd costliness; he knew the limits of his capacity for suffering.
30 Violet unlocked the door and let in the morn, and shivered at the tonic. This act of opening the shop-door, though having picked up the milk she at once closed the door again, seemed to mark another stage in the process which Elsie had begun more than two hours earlier; it broke the spell of night by letting in not only the morn but dailiness. She gathered the envelopes
35 together from the floor, and noticed one with a halfpenny stamp, which she immediately opened—furtively. Yes, it was the gas bill for the September quarter, the quarter which ought to be the lightest of the year. And was not! She deciphered the dread total; it affected her like an accusation of crime,

like an impeachment for treason. She felt guilty, yet she had done her utmost
to 'keep the gas down'. What would Henry say?

'Elsie', said Violet, peeping into the bathroom on her way upstairs. 'Do
you really need that geyser full on all the time?' She spoke with nervous
exasperation.

'Well, 'm——'

'I don't know what your master will say when he sees the gas-bill that's
come in this very moment. I really don't. I daren't show it him.' She warningly
produced the impeachment.

'Well, 'm, I've nearly finished.' And Elsie dramatically turned off the
gas-tap of the geyser.

The gloomy bathroom was like a tropic. Linen hung sodden and heavy
along the line. And Elsie's face and arms were like bedewed beetroot. But to
Violet the excessive warmth was very pleasant.

'You didn't have any tea this morning', said she, for she had noticed that
nobody had been into the kitchen before herself.

'No, 'm. It's no use. If I'm to get through with my work Monday mornings
I can't waste my time getting my tea.'

Elsie, her brow puckered, seemed to be actually accusing her mistress of
trying to tempt her from the path of virtue. The contract between employers
and employed in that house had long since passed, so far as the employed
was concerned, far beyond the plane of the commercial. The employers gave
£20 a year; the employed gave all her existence, faculties, energy; and gave
them with passion, without reserve open or secret, without reason, sublimely.

Henry was waiting for Violet at the parlour table. He wore his overcoat.
In this manner, at his instigation, they proved on chilly mornings that they
could ignore the outrageous exactions of coal trusts and striking colliers.

1 Elsie's morning tasks are said by the author to be like an act of
  A recuperation
  B resuscitation
  C rejuvenation
  D redemption
  E rehabilitation

2 During the night hours the house is said to resemble a
  A cage
  B cellar
  C castle
  D camp
  E cave

3 'nocturnal' (line 2) means
  A painted in gloomy colours
  B hidden in evening mists
  C quiet as gentle piano music
  D belonging to the night
  E repulsive as a corpse

4 'The dawn helped' (line 4) to
  A wake Violet and Henry
  B light up Elsie's work
  C bring the house to life
  D cheer up the occupants
  E create warmth and birdsong

5 Elsie is said to linger 'naughtily' at the window (line 6) because she is normally
  A indolent
  B neglectful
  C flirtatious
  D unprincipled
  E scrupulous

6 'Conscience pricked her' (line 8) implies that Elsie feels
  A frozen
  B depressed
  C hurt
  D guilty
  E bored

7 'Conscience pricked her' (line 8) is best described as a
A metaphor
B simile
C proverb
D pun
E motto

8 'rivalled Greenwich in exactitude' (lines 11–12) means
A tried to outdo the smartness of the Royal Naval College, Greenwich
B equalled the efficiency of the Royal Observatory, Greenwich
C matched in neatness the Naval Museum, Greenwich
D competed in precision with the mean-time recorder at Greenwich
E ran contrary to the hours of the tide at Greenwich

9 In Elsie's estimation the main flaw with the parlour clock was that it
A would slide slowly along the sideboard top
B had a rather evil appearance that frightened her
C demanded as much attention as the clock at Greenwich
D measured time in a way contrary to her desires
E was unpredictable in its mechanical reliability

10 Elsie's 'great life-work' (line 17) consisted of
A washing the linen
B waking the family
C laying the table
D opening the shop
E running the household

11 The dilemma that chiefly engrosses Elsie in her work is how to
A stop worrying unduly over trifles
B wash the linen under primitive conditions
C make the clock show the correct time
D provide room for all the household's goods
E find sufficient time for all her jobs

12 Elsie is convinced that the result of her falling 'short of her ideal in labour' (lines 20–1) would be
A universal catastrophe
B wholesale destruction
C natural disgrace
D infinite suffering
E widespread distress

continue overleaf

13 The vacuum-cleaning (line 25) causes Henry deep suffering because it is

A inconvenient

B expensive

C deafening

D inefficient

E hygienic

14 Compared with Henry, Violet is

A fastidious

B lamentable

C exasperating

D wicked

E affected

15 'deprecated' (line 26) could best be replaced by

A shrugged off

B shouted down

C ignored completely

D disapproved of

E complied with

16 'dailiness' (line 34) is best replaced by

A cleaners

B tedium

C homeliness

D newspapers

E routine

17 The best clue that the passage is set in 1920s' London is the reference to

A Elsie's primitive washing methods

B the gradual accumulation of dirt

C coal trusts and striking miners

D the postage rate for gas bills

E shop owners possessing a maid

18 'the path of virtue' (line 58) in Elsie's eyes seems to be

A utter cleanliness

B self-denial

C unceasing toil

D complete honesty

E personal purity

19 Elsie's part of the 'contract between employers and employed' (lines 58–9) appears to be a state of
- **A** unquestioning poverty
- **B** exalted emotions
- **C** obvious exhaustion
- **D** decent activity
- **E** voluntary enslavement

20 Overall, Henry's character can best be described as
- **A** rapacious
- **B** fastidious
- **C** pretentious
- **D** punctilious
- **E** parsimonious

Passage Two

The name 'physiotherapy' is derived from Greek words and implies the use of physical means in the treatment of injury and disease. The curative value of some of these physical means was known to the ancient Greeks, who used massage and gymnastics not only to develop the body and maintain health
5 but also as remedial treatments. The writings of the Greek physician Hippocrates show how well the uses of massage and movement were understood. In this country, although massage has probably been used to some extent since Anglo-Saxon times, physiotherapy has become an organized profession only within the last sixty years. At the time of the foundation of the first
10 professional organization in 1895 the work consisted primarily of massage and medical gymnastics, and membership was at first restricted to women, but in 1920 men were admitted to membership and have since joined the profession in increasing numbers. With the discovery that electric currents could be used in the treatment of disease the scope of the work increased.
15 Physiotherapists work in the physiotherapy department of the wards of a hospital or in a rehabilitation centre under the supervision of a superintendent physiotherapist. The treatment is given under the direction of the medical staff. Occasionally treatment is given to patients in their own homes if they are too ill or disabled to come to the hospital. The work is very varied; no
20 two patients are alike and a physiotherapist is responsible for administering a wide range of treatment.

Massage—the manipulation of the soft tissues of the body which helps to improve the circulation of the blood—is used to relieve pain and relax muscles, and to improve their function. It is given usually in combination
25 with movements, in the treatment of fractures, stiff joints, soft tissue injuries, and some forms of paralysis. Remedial gymnastics is treatment by active exercise with or without the use of apparatus. Patients may receive remedial exercise in bed, in a physiotherapy treatment room, or a gymnasium. Some patients may be able to do fairly strenuous physical exercise while others will
30 have to be encouraged by the physiotherapist to perform very simple movements. Some will perhaps have to be taught to walk again after illness or accident, while others may need special exercises either before or after operations. All the exercises are planned to help the patient to carry out everyday activities and to be as independent as possible. Electrotherapy, too, is used
35 for a variety of purposes—to ease pain, to assist the healing of wounds, and to maintain or restore the strength of muscles. A physiotherapy department is equipped with a range of apparatus for the application of various electrical currents and rays in the treatment of disease. The ancients knew the healing

value of the sun's rays but not how they worked and they could not rely on
40 the sun shining when needed for treatment any more than we can today. The
apparatus used by modern physiotherapists generates the heat rays and the
ultra-violet rays of the sun's spectrum at the turn of a switch, and these are
applied in just the right strength to produce the maximum benefit.

The work demands good powers of observation; it is important for physio-
45 therapists and remedial gymnasts to notice and report accurately on their
patients' progress.

1 The second element of the word 'physio*therapy*' (line 1) essentially means

A remedy
B physique
C disease
D massage
E gymnastics

2 In England physiotherapeutic massage was first used

A in Hippocrates's time
B before 1895
C in 1895
D in 1920
E after 1920

3 Physiotherapy includes

  I the manipulation of the body
 II active exercise
III the dispensing of medicines
IV the repair of fractures
 V the use of electrical currents

A I, II, and IV only
B I, II, and V only
C II, III, and IV only
D II, IV, and V only
E III, IV, and V only

4 When the professional organization for physiotherapists began its members were all

A masseurs
B gymnasts
C doctors
D men
E women

5 A 'rehabilitation centre' (line 16) is primarily

A an out-patients' department
B a borstal institution
C an ex-servicemen's centre
D a convalescent home
E a recuperative unit

6 The treatment given by a physiotherapist is decided by

   A himself
   B his superintendent
   C the hospital board
   D a doctor
   E the patient

7 The physiotherapist may find himself working in all of the following EXCEPT

   A hospital wards
   B casualty departments
   C hospital units
   D special remedial centres
   E patients' homes

8 Massage can relieve pain primarily by

   A toning up the muscles
   B dealing with stiff joints
   C improving blood-circulation
   D working on the soft tissues
   E inducing relaxation

9 A physiotherapist must adapt his treatment to the position of

   A himself
   B his apparatus
   C his patient
   D the doctor
   E the hospital

10 Physiotherapy is used primarily to make patients

   A more agile in the gymnasium
   B less reliant on others
   C more able to bear strain
   D less troublesome to doctors
   E more able to attend hospital

11 The passage suggests that electricity is used in physiotherapy for all of the following EXCEPT

   A reducing the amount of pain bearable
   B making the patient more comfortable
   C accelerating the process of healing
   D stopping the deterioration of muscles
   E restoring strength to weak muscles

continue overleaf

12 'generates' (line 41) means

A uses

B increases

C filters

D produces

E moderates

13 The Greeks fully understood the healing properties of

A the weather

B the sun's rays

C ultra-violet light

D the sun's spectrum

E electrical currents

14 In modern physiotherapy machines enable the sun's rays to be

A controlled

B simulated

C harnessed

D stimulated

E isolated

15 The passage suggests that a physiotherapist must be

   I detached

  II perceptive

III precise

IV progressive

  V sensitive

A I and II only

B I and III only

C II and III only

D II and V only

E IV and V only

16 It is never suggested that physiotherapy can be used in the treatment of

A broken legs

B flesh wounds

C painful joints

D brain injuries

E paralysis

17 Physiotherapy uses methods of treatment that are essentially

   A chemical

   B electrical

   C psychological

   D physical

   E synthetic

18 The main argument of the whole passage is

   A a plea for better physiotherapy facilities

   B a history of healing by natural means

   C a discussion of the value of physiotherapy

   D a defence of remedial physical exercises

   E an outline of physiotherapeutic methods

19 The writer does not suggest that the physiotherapist shares responsibility with doctors for

   A alleviating suffering

   B observing symptoms

   C treating injuries

   D diagnosing illnesses

   E curing diseases

20 The style of the passage can best be described as

   A imaginative

   B discursive

   C descriptive

   D argumentative

   E ornate

Answer all questions. Do not guess.

Passage One

The music resumed. He listened, ready to put himself into the mood of admiration if it was the Glazounov item. Was it Glazounov? He could not be certain. It sounded fine. Surely it sounded Russian. Then he had a glimpse of a programme held by a man standing near, and he peered at it. 'No. 4.
5 Elgar—Sea-Pictures.' No. 5 was the Glazounov.

'It's only the Elgar', he said, with careless condescension, perceiving at once, by the mere virtue of a label, that the music was not fine and not Russian.

The Glazounov ballet music, *The Seasons*, started. Knowing himself to be justified, he surrendered to it, to its exoticism, to its Russianism, to its wilful
10 and disconcerting beauty. And they were all beautiful beneath the music. The music softened; the fountain was heard; the striking of matches was heard. . . . Still, all was beautiful. Then he touched Marguerite's hand as it rested a little behind her on the ledge. The music grew louder, and as it were under cover of the music he put his hand round her hand. It was a venture-
15 some act with such a girl; he was afraid. . . . The hand lay acquiescent; it accepted. The flushing realization of her compliance overwhelmed him.

The applause at the end of the number awoke him. He released her hand. She slipped neatly down from the ledge.

'I think I ought to be going back home . . . Father . . .' she murmured.
20 She met his eyes; but his embarrassed eyes would not meet hers.

'Certainly!' he agreed quickly, 'but I'll see you again tomorrow morning!' and he took her home to Turnham Green.

Next morning the roads were covered with a very even, very thin coating of mud; it was as though a corps of highly skilled house-painters had laid on
25 the mud, and just vanished. The pavements had a kind of yellowish-brown varnish. The sky was of blue-black with golden rents and gleams that travelled steadily eastwards. Except the man with newspapers at the corner of Alexandra Grove, scarcely a sign of life showed along the vistas of Fulham Road; but the clock over the jeweller's was alive and bearing the usual false witness. From
30 the upper open galleries of the Workhouse one or two old men and old women in uniform looked down indifferently upon the free world which they had left for ever. George crossed the road on his way towards Redcliffe Gardens and Earl's Court. He was very smart, indeed smarter than ever, having produced in himself quite naturally and easily a fair imitation of the elegant figures which,
35 upon his visits to the restaurant-building in Piccadilly, he had observed airing themselves round about Bond Street. His hair was like polished marble; his overcoat was new, the spots of colour in his attire complied with the operative decrees. His young face had in it nothing that obviously separated him from

the average youth of his clothes. Nobody would have said of him, at a glance, that he might be a particularly serious individual. And most people would have at once classed him as a callow pleasure-seeking person in the act of seeking pleasure.

No cloud would have obscured the inward radiance caused by the lovely image of Marguerite and by his confidence in himself, had it not been for his criticisms of the world. He had moods of being rather gravely concerned as to the world, and as to London. He was recovering from the first great attack of London. He saw faults in London. Upon this Sunday morning, he was positively pained by the aspect of Redcliffe Gardens. The Redcliffe Arms public-house, locked and dead, which was the daily paradise of hundreds of human-beings, and had given balm and illusion to whole generations, seemed simply horrible to him in its Sunday morning coma. And the Redcliffe Arms was the true gate to the stucco and areas of Redcliffe Gardens. He looked down into the areas and saw therein the furtive existence of squalor behind barred windows. All the obscene apparatus of London life was there. And as he raised his eyes to the drawing-room and bedroom storeys he found no relief. His eyes could discover nothing that was not mean, ugly, frowzy, and un-imaginative. He pictured the heavy, gloomy, lethargic life within. The slatternly servants pottering about the bases of the sooty buildings sickened and sad-dened him. A solitary Earl's Court omnibus that lumbered past with its sinister, sparse cargo seemed to be a spectacle absolutely tragic—he did not know why. The few wayfarers were obviously prim and smug. No joy, no elegance, anywhere! Only, at intervals, a feeling that mysterious and repulsive wealth was hiding itself like an ogre in the eternal twilight of a fastness beyond the stuccoed walls and the grimy curtains. . . . The city worked six days in order to be precisely this on the seventh.

1 Marguerite and George spend most of their evening together at a
    A film show
    B ballet performance
    C art gallery
    D symphony concert
    E stage play

2 George's knowledge of music is best described as
    A sensitive
    B non-existent
    C hesitant
    D specialized
    E profound

3 'careless condescension' (line 6) is best replaced by
    A patronizing lack of concern
    B foolish sense of inferiority
    C aloofness free from worry
    D thoughtless paying of respect
    E clumsy attempts at affability

4 'virtue' (line 7) means
    A purity
    B strength
    C integrity
    D excellence
    E decency

5 George allows himself to enjoy the Glazounov ballet music only when he
    A is sitting comfortably
    B is certain of its title
    C can clearly see the ballet
    D has lit a cigarette
    E has obtained a programme

6 'exoticism' (line 9) means
    A mystery
    B volume
    C strangeness
    D elegance
    E excitement

7 'they were all beautiful beneath the music' (line 10) because
  A the audience was composed of handsome men and women
  B the orchestra became enraptured as they played
  C the ballet dancers moved gracefully to the music
  D the pictures were embellished by the musical accompaniment
  E the music involved the audience in its lovely world

8 Marguerite's reaction to George's taking her hand shows that she
  A adored him
  B liked him
  C was indifferent to him
  D disliked him
  E was angry with him

9 During the last part of *The Seasons* George is
  A dreaming about Marguerite
  B enjoying the Glazounov music
  C feeling physically uncomfortable
  D looking rather handsome
  E smoking a cigarette

10 Marguerite's behaviour during the evening together is best described as
  A irritated
  B bored
  C composed
  D excited
  E perplexed

11 During the evening together George experiences all the following feelings
EXCEPT
  A apprehension
  B rapture
  C confusion
  D disappointment
  E confidence

12 The muddy roads (lines 23–4) are said to look as if they have been painted
by experienced decorators because they are
  A uniformly spread
  B completely empty
  C yellowish-brown
  D highly varnished
  E neatly finished

continue overleaf

13 The clock over the jeweller's (line 29) is

    A stopped at the correct time

    B adorned with characters from fiction

    C supporting strange moving figures

    D showing the time inaccurately

    E full of hidden danger from electricity

14 Living in the Workhouse (lines 30–2) obviously entails

    I wearing its livery

    II living permanently upstairs

    III being elderly

    IV working on Sunday

    V giving up some freedom

    A I, II and III only

    B I, III and V only

    C II, III and IV only

    D II, IV and V only

    E III, IV and V only

15 George's hair is said to resemble 'polished marble' (line 36) mainly because it is

    A black

    B shiny

    C costly

    D stiff

    E rounded

16 'complied with the operative decrees' (lines 37–8) means

    A obeyed the legal regulations in force

    B would have matched his working clothes

    C conformed to the rules then applying

    D would have involved him in a divorce scandal

    E gained him a university award

17 The 'balm and illusion' dispensed by the Redcliffe Arms (line 50) is composed mostly of

    A companionship and conversation

    B music and entertainment

    C food and warmth

    D drink and happiness

    E song and laughter

18 The Redcliffe Arms is said to be like a person in a coma (line 51) because it seems to be

A dead

B asleep

C inert

D stupefied

E silent

19 Wealth is compared to an ogre in a fastness (lines 62–3) because it is all of the following EXCEPT

A powerful

B apprehensive

C concealed

D odious

E incomprehensible

20 George's mood as he walks through Redcliffe Gardens can best be described as

A exasperated

B romantic

C disillusioned

D bewildered

E passionate

Passage Two

The first recorded attempt to explain the creation and composition of the heavenly bodies was made by the Sumerians in the third millennium B.C. The Sumerians, who inhabited a 300-mile-long realm between the Tigris and Euphrates rivers, gave to civilization the wheel, the plough and cuneiform
5 writing. As befitted such innovators, they had a conception of the universe both realistic and imaginative: a sea-girt hemisphere in which the heavenly bodies clustered in the wind above the familiar water and earth. According to Sumerian mythology, these elements were governed by the gods of creation —giants in human shape.

10 Greek philosophers subjected earlier myths concerning the universe to painstaking inquiry. Because they sought a 'first principle' as a basic cause of all phenomena, the Greeks came up with some imaginative, if inaccurate, explanations of the universe. In the sixth century B.C. the philosopher Thales reasoned that water must be the raw material from which the universe was
15 produced. Anaximander, a friend of Thales, held that the universe began with a sphere of fire enclosing a cold, moist mass, from which it was separated by a layer of mist. Eventually, the cold mass became the earth, the fire became the light of the heavenly bodies, and the mist the surrounding atmosphere. [1]

In the fifth century B.C., Philaos adopted a radically different approach
20 Believing the number 10 to signify perfection he presupposed a universe of 10 heavenly bodies. Since only 9—5 planets, the sun, the moon, the earth and the sphere of the stars—were visible, a tenth, the counter earth, was invented. Arbitrary as this system was, it was the first to picture the earth as a revolving sphere like other planets.

25 Early Greek philosophers pondered the universe with little more than their logic and eyesight to help them. But later Greeks applied maturing mathematical skills to the problem of heavenly movements. As early as the fourth century B.C., Eudoxus sought a formula to explain what appeared to be looping planetary paths. Believing that planets orbited the earth in perfect
30 circles, Eudoxus drew twenty-seven concentric spheres around the earth. Each sphere, or any body within it, was calculated to rotate on a different axis. Eudoxus could approximate the motions of the heavenly body by combining the movements of these spheres.

But Eudoxus's clever theory left unexplained why planets dimmed and grew
35 bright, indicating variations in their distance from the earth. In the first century A.D. the astronomer-cartographer Ptolemy devised a system in which planets revolved in small circles while orbiting the earth. Thus Ptolemy 'proved' that a planet might be close to the earth at one sighting and distant

at another, while its principal motion remained a circle round the earth.

40 'Although the idea seemed absurd,' wrote the famous sixteenth-century Polish astronomer, Nicolaus Copernicus, 'I began to think of a motion of the earth.' Once it was assumed that the earth itself rotated each day—rather than having all the other heavenly bodies rush around the earth every 24 hours—the motions of the planets, said Copernicus, became more comprehensible.

45 Having challenged the established notion of a fixed earth, Copernicus ventured further. In 1512 he put the sun, instead of the earth, at the centre of the solar system. However, he still believed that the planets orbited in perfect circles. It was not until 1609 that the German astronomer Johannes Kepler described the planetary paths correctly for the first time. Agreeing with

50 Copernicus that the planets were sun-centred, Kepler began to question the notion of circular orbits. His calculations, based on voluminous and precise observations, indicated elliptical orbits instead. Proceeding on this assumption, Kepler then proved that the speed of a planet depends on its distance from the sun. This finding, broadened by Newton into his gravitation law,

55 ended, once and for all, the age-old speculation on the motions of the solar system.

1 The Sumerians believed that the universe was formed by the
  A Tigris and Euphrates
  B wind over the earth
  C immense gods of creation
  D earth, air, fire, and water
  E sea-girt heavenly bodies

2 Records of men's thoughts about the composition of the universe can be traced back for about
  A 10,000 years
  B 8,000 years
  C 5,000 years
  D 3,000 years
  E 2,000 years

3 'hemisphere' (line 6) means a
  A round, flat area
  B half-circle
  C bowl-shaped universe
  D ball-shaped universe
  E circle within a circle

4 It is suggested that the theories of the universe put forward by the Sumerians and the Greeks were similar because they were both
  A improbable
  B factual
  C derivative
  D scientific
  E imaginative

5 'first principle' (line 11) means
  A moral philosophy
  B fundamental idea
  C acceptable mythology
  D plausible phenomenon
  E main thesis

6 Philaos's most important contribution to man's true knowledge of the universe was his belief that the
  A planets had elliptical paths round the earth
  B earth itself revolved on its axis
  C earth was the centre of the universe
  D sun was the centre of the solar system
  E universe had ten heavenly bodies

112

7 'radically' (line 19) means

    A fundamentally

    B completely

    C partially

    D drastically

    E rationally

8 The theory put forward by Philaos is described as 'arbitrary' (line 23) because it

    A takes all the facts into consideration

    B fails to take all the facts into consideration

    C accepts all the relevant facts except one

    D rejects all the relevant facts except one

    E accepts none of the facts

9 The variation in the light from the planets indicates that

    A their internal heat rises and falls

    B their rays vary according to their seasons

    C their rotations present differently lit sides

    D they revolve in small circles

    E their distance from the earth varies

10 Ptolemy differed from all the other astronomers named because he

    A drew maps

    B was a Greek

    C lived after Christ

    D argued scientifically

    E devised a star system

11 The word 'proved' (line 38) is in inverted commas to suggest that Ptolemy had

    A succeeded in silencing his critics

    B demonstrated his theory conclusively

    C found the right answer at last

    D failed to find the right answer

    E used this word in his own explanation

12 Copernicus first thought his own idea absurd (line 40) because it was

    A new

    B improbable

    C impossible

    D ingenious

    E unscientific

continue overleaf

13 Copernicus accepted all the following theories except that which said the

    A sun was at the centre of the universe

    B earth moved round the sun

    C planets moved in perfect circles

    D planets moved round the earth

    E earth took 24 hours to spin once

14 The use of 'rush around' (line 43) suggests that Copernicus thought that

    A the planets moved at great speed

    B the earth moved at great speed

    C earlier theories were laughable

    D his own theory was laughable

    E the universe was full of activity

15 The first astronomer to realize that the earth revolved on its own axis was

    A Copernicus

    B Eudoxus

    C Philaos

    D Thales

    E Ptolemy

16 The word 'ventured' (line 46) is used particularly to suggest that Copernicus's approach was

    A scientific

    B hesitant

    C exploratory

    D courageous

    E foolhardy

17 'elliptical' (line 52) suggests orbits that might be all of the following EXCEPT

    A circular

    B oval-shaped

    C non-circular

    D irregular

    E elongated

18 Kepler's approach differed from the approaches of earlier astronomers because it was based on

    A detailed information

    B observable fact

    C scientific theory

    D mathematical formulas

    E philosophical understanding

19 The speed of the planets around the sun is affected by their
  A distance from the sun
  B distance from the earth
  C distance from each other
  D relative size and weight
  E speed of rotation on their axes

20 Newton's law of gravity arose directly from
  A Eudoxus's theory of orbiting planets
  B Copernicus's theory of the spinning earth
  C Copernicus's theory of a sun-centred universe
  D Kepler's theory of the speed of planets
  E Kepler's theory of the planets' elliptical orbits

TEST 10

Answer all questions. Do not guess.

Passage One

The dusk was far advanced. Mounting the steps of Number 8, Manresa Road, Chelsea, quickly, Marguerite rang the bell. There was no answer. She pushed up the flap of the letter-aperture and looked within.

An adventurous idea occurred to George in a flash and he impulsively 5 adopted it. His latchkey was in his pocket, but if the house door was once opened he would lose her—he would have to go forth and seek his dinner and she would remain in the house; whereas, barred out of the house, she would be bound to him—they would be thrust together into exquisite contingencies, into all the deep potentialities of dark London.

10 'Dash it!' he said, first fumbling in both waistcoat pockets simultaneously. 'I must have left it in my other clothes.'

Before a word could be said as to the next move, a figure passed in front of the gate and then halted.

'Oh! It's Mr Buckingham Smith!' exclaimed Marguerite. 'Mr Buckingham 15 Smith, we're locked out till father comes.' She completed the tale of the mishap, to George's equal surprise and mortification.

Mr Buckingham Smith, with Mr Alfred Prince, was tenant of the studio at the back of No. 8. He raised his hat as well as an occupied arm would allow.

20 'Come and wait in the studio, then', he suggested bluntly.

'You know Mr Cannon, don't you?' said Marguerite, embarrassed.

George and Mr Buckingham Smith had in fact been introduced to one another weeks earlier. Thereafter Mr Buckingham Smith had, as George imagined, saluted George with a kind of jealous defiance and mistrust, and 25 the acquaintance had not progressed. But now Mr Buckingham Smith grew affable and neighbourly. Behind the man's inevitable insistence that George should accompany Miss Haim into the studio was a genuine, eager hospitality.

In the studio Mr Alfred Prince, whom also George knew slightly, was trimming a huge oil-lamp which depended by a wire from the scarcely visible 30 apex of the roof. When at length the natural perversity of the lamp had been mastered and the metal shade replaced, George got a general view of the immense and complex disorder of the studio. It was obviously very dirty— even in the lamplight the dust could be seen in drifts on the moveless folds of the curtains—it was a pigsty; but it was romantic with shadowed spaces, 35 and gleams of copper and of the pale arms of the etching press, and glimpses of pictures. He was glad, now, that Mr Buckingham Smith had invited them in. He had wanted to keep Marguerite Haim to himself; but it was worth while to watch her under the illumination of the lamp.

There was a pause, and Mr Prince sighed and said: 'I was thinking of
40 going up to the Promenades tonight, but Smith won't go.'

George took fire at once. 'The Glazounov ballet music?'

'Glazounov?' repeated Mr Prince uncertainly. 'Good lord, no. I rather
wanted to hear the new Elgar.'

The reception given to the wonderful name of Glazounov in that studio
45 was more than a disappointment for George; he felt obscurely that it amounted
to a snub.

He smiled sheepishly and was angry with himself. Then he heard Mr Prince
saying calmly and easily to Miss Haim—the little old man could not in fact
be so nervous as he seemed:
50 'I suppose you wouldn't come with me to the Prom?'

George was staggered and indignant. It was inconceivable, monstrous,
that those two should be on such terms as would warrant Mr Prince's astounding proposal. He felt that he simply could not endure them marching off
together for the evening. Her acceptance of the proposal would be an outrage.
55 He trembled. However, she declined, and he was lifted from the rack.

'I must really go', she said. 'Father's sure to be home by now.'

And next he was outside in the dark with Marguerite, but Mr Haim had
not returned.

'Well!' she muttered; and then dreamily: 'What a funny little man Mr
60 Prince is, isn't he?' She spoke condescendingly.

'Anyhow', said George, who had been respecting Mr Alfred Prince, 'anyhow, I'm glad you didn't go to the concert with him.'

'Why?' she asked, with apparent simplicity. 'I adore the Proms. Don't you?'

'Let's go, then', he suggested. 'We shan't be very late, and what else is there
65 for you to do?'

His audacity frightened him. There she stood with him in the porch, silent,
reflective. She would never go. For sundry practical and other reasons she
would refuse. She must refuse.

'I'll go', she said, as if announcing a well-meditated decision. He could
70 scarcely believe it. This could not be London that he was in.

1 The best meaning of 'exquisite contingencies' (lines 8–9) is

    A agonizing restraints

    B splendid company

    C beautiful scenes

    D strange incidents

    E rich possibilities

2 'the deep potentialities of dark London' (line 9) refers to the city's

    A manifold night life

    B numerous cellar clubs

    C hidden criminal world

    D intricate underground railways

    E sinister riverside walks

3 'simultaneously' (line 10) means

    A superficially

    B concurrently

    C ludicrously

    D despondently

    E agitatedly

4 George pretends to lose his latchkey so that he

    A does not have to cook his own meal

    B can spend the evening with Marguerite

    C may take Marguerite to the 'Proms'

    D has the opportunity to visit the studio

    E is able to meet Mr Buckingham Smith

5 Mr Smith 'saluted George with a kind of jealous defiance and mistrust' (line 24) probably because he was

    A only a studio tenant

    B quite unsure of himself

    C much poorer than George

    D another admirer of Marguerite

    E a rival artist

6 On this occasion Mr Smith is 'affable' and 'neighbourly' (line 26) due, probably, to his

    A desire to show his studio

    B eagerness to impress Marguerite

    C wish for Mr Haim's friendship

    D craving for more companionship

    E friendly feelings towards George

7 George's major impressions of the studio are that it is
  A large, grimy but well-lit
  B jumbled, filthy but wonderful
  C squalid, old-fashioned but organized
  D lofty, sordid but uninteresting
  E confused, cramped but luxurious

8 The 'Promenades' referred to in line 40 are
  A seaside walks
  B shopping areas
  C parkland avenues
  D musical concerts
  E ballet performances

9 Because Mr Prince preferred Elgar to Glazounov, George feels
  A slightly foolish and self-doubting
  B rather bored and self-deprecating
  C somewhat astonished and self-critical
  D faintly amused and self-aware
  E vaguely rebuffed and self-reproachful

10 George 'took fire' (line 41) means that he
  A was also bathed in lamplight
  B became irritated with Mr Smith
  C felt rejected by the others
  D grew full of sudden enthusiasm
  E had a growing passion for Marguerite

11 George is 'staggered and indignant' (line 51) when he hears Mr Prince invite Marguerite to go to the Prom, mainly because
  A Mr Prince was a little old man
  B Mr Haim would be worried about her
  C Mr Smith's hospitality would be rebuffed
  D George planned to have her to himself
  E Marguerite is the artist's social superior

12 George is said to resemble a man being 'lifted from the rack' (line 55) since he is no longer
  A suffering anxiety
  B feeling sick
  C under pressure
  D fully stretched
  E tied down

continue overleaf

13 'condescendingly' (line 60) means
  A irritably
  B quietly
  C patronizingly
  D affably
  E obligingly

14 George respects Mr Prince mainly because he
  A is a good pictorial artist
  B prefers Elgar's music to Glazounov's
  C seems much older than George
  D does not care about appearances
  E shows no fear of Marguerite

15 Marguerite's 'simplicity' is 'apparent' (line 63) because she
  A is a distinctly naive girl
  B knows George really likes her
  C is easy to get on with
  D makes an obviously sincere enquiry
  E states her questions very clearly

16 George's 'audacity frightened him' (line 66) most probably because
  A it was dangerous in the dark streets
  B Marguerite disliked his proposed destination
  C Mr Haim would be furious at their absence
  D Mr Prince had already been rebuffed
  E he had not dared to ask her out before

17 'She would never go. . . . She must refuse' (lines 67–8) are words representing
  A George's reported speech
  B Marguerite's reported speech
  C the author's reported comments
  D George's reported thoughts
  E Marguerite's reported thoughts

18 Until Marguerite's acceptance of his invitation, George's feelings for her do not seem to have been
  A ardent
  B honourable
  C obvious
  D reciprocated
  E desperate

19 George feels that he cannot be in London (line 70) because the city
  A was so dark and silent
  B did not really give Promenades
  C felt like an utter paradise
  D ended well before Manresa Road
  E is not this story's setting

20 The style of this passage is best described as
  A sarcastic
  B argumentative
  C scientific
  D humorous
  E philosophical

Passage Two

Vineyards in France collectively occupy only $3\frac{1}{2}$ million acres, but locally, where they may constitute a monoculture, they are of considerable importance. Vines were once grown in certain areas which have now abandoned them for other forms of agriculture. This was true of both Normandy and the Charente
5 regions, where a traditional association of wine and cheese has now given way to a more exclusively dairying pattern. Looking at the agricultural landscape of Normandy today, it is easy to forget that vines were once grown to the north of what is sometimes said to be the northern limit of vine cultivation in France, i.e. a line stretching from the lower Loire to the Ardennes. Clearly
10 this present-day limit is an economic rather than a botanical one. The phylloxera disease which devastated many French vineyards in the late nineteenth century has also had a lasting effect upon the distribution pattern. Certain areas, such as the Charentes, never recovered their former importance. Others, like the flat coastlands of Languedoc, acquired a new significance, for here the
15 vinestock could be artificially flooded, this being one of the devices used to control the disease.

Yields of wine tend to decrease from south to north whereas quality increases in the same direction. This is a useful generalization although it is a crude one and many exceptions can be found to it. The difference in yield
20 between south and north—a typical vineyard in Hérault may give ten times the yield per acre of one in Burgundy—is largely a consequence of the way in which the vines are grown. In the north, care is taken to choose sunny slopes for vineyards, but despite this the individual vines are generally planted farther apart than in the south in order to catch the maximum sunlight.
25 Branches are also removed and others trained along wires for the same reason. The vintage quality of wine varies from year to year, a consequence of annual variations in climate. Regional and local climatic differences similarly affect the quality; the higher summer temperatures of the south favour a high alcoholic content in the *vin ordinaire*. The very great reputation of northern
30 wines, such as Champagne, depends more upon the skill which goes into their making than upon any special elements in the local climate.

In 1874 France produced 84 million hectolitres of wine—a record. Subsequently the phylloxera disease resulted in the destruction of acres of vineyards and production totalled only 45 million hectolitres in 1911. It was
35 during these lean years that the seeds of future competition were sown in other countries: Australia, South Africa and Algeria. Between the wars new planting with hardy American vinestock resulted in big French harvests once more, and 78 million hectolitres were produced in 1934. Since the Second

World War a total of around 60 million hectolitres has been more usual, but the volume fluctuates a good deal with season and big harvests are still recorded—73½ million hectolitres in 1962. Such bumper harvests result in a wine surplus that is only aggravated by the imports of wine from Algeria to which France is still committed by treaty. It is difficult for France to avoid buying this Algerian wine since there is little market for it in Moslem North Africa, and refusal to take it could result in reprisals over Saharan oil. In order to combat this recurrent problem of surpluses the French government has imposed restrictions on the planting of new vineyards and has placed controls on the marketing of wine. There have also been campaigns aimed at the destruction of vineyards. But the land to be abandoned will support virtually nothing else. It is unrealistic to expect the small proprietor who can make a living from an acre or two of vineyard to be able to survive on a similar acreage of grass and fodder crops.

1 Vineyards are not cultivated extensively in northern France today because
  A the climate will not allow them to grow
  B the vines there are more vulnerable to disease
  C the wine would be of very poor quality
  D sufficient quantities of wine could not be produced
  E other forms of farming are more profitable

2 Vineyards are extremely important in areas where
  A cheese is no longer made
  B wine is the only major product
  C dairying is not a viable form of farming
  D arable farming is not possible at all
  E the sun is rare and not too strong

3 'traditional' (line 5) means
  A customary
  B ancient
  C common
  D conservative
  E local

4 In the nineteenth century the phylloxera disease produced all of the following results EXCEPT
  A wine production was drastically reduced
  B areas of wine production changed
  C land was flooded to control the disease
  D diseased fields were not replanted
  E serious competition from overseas began

5 Languedoc became an important wine-growing area free from disease because
  A it was on a low-lying coast
  B the land was flat and fertile
  C the vineyards could be flooded
  D disease did not menace the vines
  E vines need large quantities of water

6 Compared with the wine crops in the south of France those produced further north generally

  I yield more
  II yield less
  III are of better quality
  IV are of poorer quality

A I and II only
B I and III only
C II and III only
D II and IV only
E III and IV only

7 Hérault gives more wine per acre than Burgundy mainly because its
A soil is more fertile
B climate is much better
C wine cultivation is different
D position is very low-lying
E slopes are more steeply terraced

8 To ensure sound crops wine-growers in the more northern areas take all
of the following measures EXCEPT
A the removal of shading branches
B the training of branches along lines
C the planting of vines spaced apart
D the selection of high-yielding vines
E the choice of special sunny slopes

9 Variations in the quality of the wine from a given area in the south depend
mainly upon the
A soil
B seasons
C weather
D harvesting
E processing

10 'vintage' (line 26) means
A standard
B individual
C ancient
D production
E alcoholic

11 For a vine to produce wine strong in alcohol it must have
A strong sunlight
B hot summers
C adequate water
D rich terrain
E strong fertilizers

continue overleaf

12 The bulk of French wine production today depends on vines brought
originally from
  A Australia
  B Languedoc
  C America
  D Normandy
  E Algeria

13 A 'hectolitre' (line 32) consists of
  A 10 litres
  B 100 litres
  C 500 litres
  D 1000 litres
  E 10,000 litres

14 The 'lean years' (line 35) is a well-known English phrase taken from a
story found in
  A The Bible
  B *Pilgrim's Progress*
  C *Julius Caesar*
  D *Tom Sawyer*
  E The Koran

15 'seeds' (line 35) refer figuratively to
  A troubles
  B vines
  C beginnings
  D offshoots
  E ideas

16 Since the devastations caused by the phylloxera disease the largest French
wine harvest occurred in
  A 1874
  B 1911
  C 1934
  D 1958
  E 1962

17 'aggravated' (line 42) means
  A irritated
  B enervated
  C ameliorated
  D extenuated
  E exacerbated

18 France imports large quantities of Algerian wine mainly because
   A the wine is of a very high quality
   B it cannot produce enough itself
   C Moslems are not allowed to drink wine
   D French colonialists planted the vines
   E it is bound by a mutual trade pact

19 Compared with the land required for viniculture that needed for dairy farming is proportionately
   A more
   B less
   C richer
   D poorer
   E identical

20 The subject discussed in this passage is approached essentially from the standpoint of
   A a farmer
   B a historian
   C a geographer
   D an entomologist
   E a horticulturalist

ACKNOWLEDGMENTS

For permission to use copyright material in this book, the authors and publishers wish to thank the following:

the owner of the copyright and Messrs Methuen & Co Ltd for an extract from *The Card* by Arnold Bennett; Messrs Laurence Pollinger Ltd and the estate of the late Mrs Frieda Lawrence for two extracts from *The White Peacock* by D. H. Lawrence; Yale University Press for an extract from *Life of the Past* by George Gaylord Simpson, copyright © 1953 Yale University Press; Mr Sean O'Faolain for an extract from 'The Judas Touch' (from *The Finest Short Stories of Sean O'Faolain*); Messrs Routledge & Kegan Paul Ltd for an extract from *A History of Shopping* by Dorothy Davis; Mr Howard Spring and Messrs William Collins, Sons & Co Ltd, for an extract from *Fame Is the Spur*; Mr T. C. Willett and Messrs Tavistock Publications Ltd for an extract from *Criminal on the Road*; Messrs A. D. Peters & Co for an extract from 'The Man of the House' (from *Travellers' Samples*) by Frank O'Connor; Messrs Thames & Hudson Ltd for an extract from *From Peace to War* by M. G. Bruce; Mrs Cheston Bennett, the owner of the copyrights, for an extract from *Lilian* by Arnold Bennett; Messrs Penguin Books Ltd for an extract from *Water in the Service of Man* by H. R. Vallentine; Miss Iris Murdoch and Messrs Chatto & Windus Ltd for an extract from *Flight from the Enchanter*; Messrs Penguin Books Ltd for an extract from *Chemistry* by Kenneth Hutton; Grolier Inc for an extract from 'How to Look at Art' (from *The Book of Art*, volume 10); the owner of the copyright and Messrs Cassell & Co for an extract from *Riceyman Steps* by Arnold Bennett; the Controller of Her Majesty's Stationery Office for an extract from *Physiotherapy* ('Choice of Careers', number 52); Mrs Cheston Bennett, the owner of the copyrights, for two extracts from *The Roll Call* by Arnold Bennett; Time-Life Books for an extract from *The Planets* (*Life* 'Science Library' volume) by Carl Sagan and Jonathan Norton Leonard, copyright © 1965 Time Inc; Messrs Macmillan & Co Ltd for an extract from *Economic Geography of France* by D. I. Scargill.